WORSHIP&
DAILY
LIFE

A Resource for Worship Planners

Introduction by
Doris Rudy

D1636959

DISCIPLESHIP RESOURCES

P.O. BOX 840 • NASHVILLE, TENNESSEE 37202-0840

www.discipleshipresources.org

WORSHIP&
DAILY
LIFE

Cover and book design by Sharon Anderson

ISBN 0-88177-245-3

Library of Congress Card Catalog No. 98-70466

DR245

Contents

**WORSHIP &
DAILY
LIFE**

Introduction
by Doris J. Rudy

It was Teacher Recognition Sunday at the church. Church school teachers, their assistants, the Education Ministry Group, and the children stood near the front of the sanctuary. Those to be recognized wore the usual red carnation for easy identification. The teachers were called by name, and an appropriate certificate of appreciation was presented to each. A number of people were missing from the scene. Professors at the nearby university and colleges, high school and elementary school teachers and administrators, seminary faculty and staff were not among the honored ones that day. I wondered, *Why were they not included?*

When it came time for the congregation to share joys and concerns, I offered thanks for *all* the educators in our congregation and for their contributions to our community through the several educational institutions. These people were then asked to stand, and the pastor named them during the pastoral prayer.

Following the service that morning, a tenured professor at Northwestern University caught up with me in the hall. "Thank you, Doris, for including me in the community prayers today," she said. "That's the first time in my twenty years in this congregation that my contributions at the university have been noted in worship here. It means a lot to me to have it done on this particular Sunday."

What happened during the service of worship on that Sunday may have had meaning only to the professor and me. I suspect that, were I to remind any number of people of that service, few would remember what occurred. The professor's words to me following the service conveyed more than her appreciation. They expressed the longing of many laity to have their work and their daily lives validated, recognized, and supported by the institutional church.

A story from my childhood illustrates another aspect of the connection between faith and daily life. My early years were spent on a farm in southern Ohio. As soon as we children were considered old enough, one of our spring chores—though it seemed more like fun then—was to help Dad plant the garden, which was his pride and joy (next to us four children, of course). A lifelong asthmatic condition forced Dad to do office work for pay and prevented his being the full-time farmer he really wanted to be, so the garden was important to him.

I remember the care with which Dad cultivated the ground, built hills for the potatoes, and dropped each seed, just so, into the carefully dug holes. We kids were taught how to place the seed-potatoes into the indented earth with the eyes upward "so they could see to grow," as Dad told us.

Gardening was clearly a worshipful experience for Dad. It was also his work. His partnership with God in that creative process nurtured their relationship. Dad's dependence on God was obvious in all that he did, but particularly in the garden-growing, when, after the planting was done, he would remark, "Only God can provide what it needs now—rain and sunshine." When he walked up and down the rows, bending slowly to cover a tender plant one of us kids had not-so-carefully dropped, or checking to see if we had placed the seeds just the right distance apart, even we novice gardeners knew the meaning of the experience for him.

The significance of Dad's garden reached far beyond whatever bond it gave him with God. Our family of six was fed for a whole year by the fruits of their partnership. What could be more worshipful?

Followers of Christ, specifically the people in the pew—the laity—spend most of their time outside the institutional church, in the world. The workplace, the home, the community and neighborhood, and the global community are the places of our daily lives. These are the contexts of our ministry as parents, firefighters, realtors, students, teachers, construction workers, composers, artists, librarians, sanitation workers, secretaries, physicians, farmers, public servants, and child-care givers. These are the places where we live out our discipleship. Making the connection between our faith and what happens in the daily places of our lives is not easy.

A few years back, the Center for the Ministry of the Laity, then located at Andover Newton School of Theology in Massachusetts, produced an image that illustrates the gap between our faith and our daily lives. A stick figure of a person stands with one foot on each side of a deep ditch. On one side of the ditch stands an office building, a factory, a school, a house, all covered by a dark cloud. Across the ditch stands a building with a cross on top. A sun shines down on this building—the church. One hand of the person is firmly fixed in and touching the everyday buildings. The other outstretched hand is *not quite* reaching the building with the cross on top! We are not quite able to link our faith to the weekday places of our lives!

That is too often the way it is with people of faith. And the gap between our faith and our daily lives shows very few signs of closing. One part of our lives is secular; another part is sacred. The former is frequently identified with evil and

WORSHIP & DAILY LIFE

corruption, overcast by dark clouds of cynicism and confusion. It constitutes the profane. It is the place from which we happily withdraw every Friday, not to think about again until Monday morning. It is those places in which we don't dare think or talk about God or faith or anything "religious."

We long to be part of that which is sacred, that which is of God, holy and mysterious—all that is good and safe and compassionate, all that is worthy. The sun always shines on that which we call sacred! It is full of stained-glass windows that cut the sun's glare and soften the harsh shadows.

The gap between the sacred and the secular is appropriate, we believe. It is seemingly insurmountable anyway, so we may as well get used to it. It makes life a lot less frightening and a whole lot safer and supports our notion that ministry is done in the church by church professionals. It relieves us of our responsibility for making a difference in the world. It lets us off the hook, so to speak, of taking seriously the biblical mandate to

> . . . bring good news to the poor.
> . . . to proclaim release to the captives
> and recovery of sight to the blind,
> to let the oppressed go free. (Luke 4:18)

We North American Christians have ways of separating our "church lives" and our "daily lives." We designate portions of our entire wardrobes as Sunday clothes, because we consider them to be newer or nicer or fancier than the clothes we wear the rest of the week. Our coworkers would want to know what was going on if we were to wear those clothes to our daily workplaces. Maybe they are too physically (or psychologically) restrictive for workday activities.

The language of faith says that we are to live by grace; yet we know that in our places of work, *merit* is the primary evaluative term. Paul Johnson, in the book *Grace: God's Work Ethic* (Judson Press, 1985), reported research done with a group of four hundred farmers, business people, nurses, school teachers, mechanics, doctors, painters, lawyers, computer operators, and secretaries who were exploring the gap between their Sunday and Monday worlds. They were asked to choose from a list of descriptive words those heard most often in church and those heard most often at work. Ninety-six percent of the respondents named *grace* as the word most often heard in church. The word most often heard in the workplace, they said, was *efficiency* (heard by seventy-seven percent of the respondents). Running a close second, third, and fourth were *performance*, *earn*, and *produce*.

The reality of the weekday world robs us of the language

of faith and adds credence to the fact that Christians need to link their daily lives with their faith lives. Without the linkage, worship becomes irrelevant to those who seek to live whole, rather than segmented, lives. Christians then easily replace Sunday worship with a leisurely morning at home or other activities.

As Christians we are called to wear the "clothes" of our everyday lives into worship and to wear our "Sunday clothes" to work, for we seek to worship God with our whole lives. We seek ways to connect our work on Monday with the work of the people on Sunday.

Liturgy—What People Do All Day

A look at liturgy would seemingly take us into the realm of the sacred, wouldn't it? Most laypeople understand the word *liturgy* to mean what we do in worship every Sunday. We talk about writing liturgy and understand it to be the words that accompany our acts of worship. The liturgist, sometimes a layperson, is the person who leads worship or reads what has been written (frequently by the pastor) for the time of worship.

Most laity in workshops I lead on this subject are surprised to learn the root meaning of the word. The word *liturgy* is actually a transliteration of the Greek word *leitourgia*, which in turn is a combination of two Greek words, *laos* (originally translated "the people of God") and *ergon*, from which we get *erg*, a unit of work (as you may have learned in high school physics). Together, *laos* and *erg* mean the people's work, or the work of the people, as it is more commonly explained. Liturgy, then, is what people do all day!

According to biblical scholars, the Greek usage of the word *leitourgia* had nothing to do with religion or the church or theology or any rites or rituals. Paul, for example, in his letter to the church in Rome, uses a closely related word, *leitourgoi*, (meaning servants or ministers) to describe the tax collectors. They were part of the government, and their work was to run the "IRS" of the Roman Empire as efficiently as possible. This revelation might even lead us to think that *liturgy* describes the work of bank tellers, parents, nurses, architects, construction workers, cobblers, dry cleaners, firefighters, government officials, recyclers, and waiters!

The connection of life and liturgy, of worship and work, of ministry and daily life is not an easy one to make. The general church population, including clergy, have seldom been helped to, or have not taken seriously the challenge to, make the connection. Service in and to the institutional church is primary in most congregations. What difference

WORSHIP & DAILY LIFE

would it make if the two were connected? More importantly, how can the connection be made?

The Scriptural Connection

We begin to make the connection by taking cue from the scriptural record, which connects life and liturgy for us. Most Bible stories are located in the daily lives of the people involved—in the fields, on the journey, outside the gates to the city, on the hillside, near the lakeshore, in the home, on the road, at dinner, in places of work, in large and small group gatherings. In Hebrew there is one word for worship and work. The Hebrews saw the two as one. God's activity in creation is focused on and in the world, in the life of the people.

Jesus' parables, healings, and teachings were set in common, everyday life situations—illness, death, decision-making, sweeping, seasoning food, buying more than is needed, trimming the lamps, boating, fishing, eating, marrying, sowing seeds, investing talents, standing with the oppressed, misplacing loyalties, and relating to family members. He used the articles of everyday life to illustrate his message. His worship was in the everyday places of people's lives. Jesus seemed to be reinforcing his understanding that the people would be engaged in his teachings through their daily lives.

An infrequently used passage in the Book of Ecclesiasticus, or The Wisdom of Ben Sira, has made it easier for me to connect my faith and my daily life. This brief section from Chapter 38 is helpful:

> How can he become wise who handles the plow . . .
> who drives oxen and is occupied with their work,
>   and whose talk is about bulls?
> He sets his heart on plowing furrows,
>   and he is careful about fodder for the heifers.
> So too is every craftsman and master workman
>   who labors by night as well as by day;
> those who cut the signets of seals,
>   each is diligent in making a great variety;
> he sets his heart on painting a lifelike image,
>   and he is careful to finish his work.
> So too is the smith sitting by the anvil,
>   intent upon his handiwork in iron;
> the breath of the fire melts his flesh,
>   and he wastes away in the heat of the furnace;
> he inclines his ear to the sound of the hammer,
>   and his eyes are on the pattern of the object.
> He sets his heart on finishing his handiwork,
>   and he is careful to complete its decoration.
> So too is the potter sitting at his work
>   and turning the wheel with his feet; . . .

he sets his heart to finish the glazing,
  and he is careful to clean the furnace.
All these rely upon their hands,
  and each is skilful [*sic*] in his own work.
Without them a city cannot be established,
  and men can neither sojourn nor live there. . . .
They keep stable the fabric of the world
  and their prayer is in the practice of their trade.

(Ecclesiasticus 38:25-32, 34;
Revised Standard Version, Apocrypha)

God gives gifts to even the humblest of laborers. They do their work diligently, careful to finish the task. They do the will of God from the heart. Their daily lives "keep stable the fabric of the world, and their prayer is in the practice of their trade." What a beautiful thought! If all of life belongs to God, then the way we live life every day is a way of talking to God—it is our prayer. It is a way of showing our concern for the world in which we live, praising God, and expressing our gratitude for life in all its fullness.

Life as Prayer

Consider the times when an action or word came to you at just the right time to provide support when you were lonely, grieving, or in what you considered a hopeless situation. Work is prayer when a letter is sent in response to a request, when a phone call is returned, when food is grown or cooked to sustain life, when repairs are made on the refrigerator, when unhealthy conditions are corrected, when vaccinations are given, when waste is recycled appropriately, when surgery is performed to save a life. Work is prayer when a loan is provided for a family to purchase their first home, when creeks and rivers are cleared of rubbish, when a visitor arrives in the hospital room.

When work is done well, it is prayer. When the pilot lands the plane safely, it is prayer—more than those prayers spoken by the passengers! When teachers use every ability they have to help children learn, it is prayer. When a friend shows concern about potentially destructive behavior, it is prayer. And when a preacher delivers a carefully prepared sermon with commitment, passion, and compassion, it is prayer.

Paul's directive to "pray without ceasing" (1 Thessalonians 5:17) has been troublesome to many Christians. Interpreted quantitatively, one would be expected to pray all the time; and that is impossible. People simply have too much else to do. Paul knew that. We are helped to understand what Paul meant by considering this injunction alongside another

WORSHIP& DAILY LIFE

piece of Paul's advice, "Present your bodies as a living sacrifice, holy and acceptable to God, which is your spiritual worship" (Romans 12:1). If we understand the word *body* to include our total being, then prayer becomes a lifestyle and not a posture requiring a bowed head. Life is prayer.

Ministry of Presence and Reconciliation

A recent video entitled *Day by Day* depicts ways in which life is presence and reconciliation. The locale is a factory assembly line where the workers do the same routine hour after hour, day after day. Into that monotony, one worker brings a birthday cake for a coworker, places it on the conveyor belt, and provides an opportunity for celebration. A simple act, but an important act of presence and reconciliation for that unrecognized worker.

When one spends time listening to coworkers, neighbors, and family members and showing concern for those who are having a difficult time, life is presence and reconciliation. Sometimes the work of the people means being very sensitive to cultural and ethnic differences in the workplace and taking the time required to bridge the gaps created by different approaches to work and differing gifts in the workplace. The work of the people at other times means identifying symptoms of workaholism in ourselves (and others) and taking steps to bring balance to our own lives.

Ministry as Creation

One way to evaluate the extent of our life as liturgy is to frequently ask the question, "How does what I'm doing contribute to God's ongoing creation?" If we can't answer the question, we need to take a serious look at our life. Think of your own life. How does it contribute to God's ongoing creation?

Working in a factory that makes parts for tractors is creation. Putting paint on a house that provides shelter for its occupants is creation. Writing news stories in a sensitive, truthful, caring way is creation. Providing legal assistance for people who have been wrongly accused is creation. Providing facilities in which people care for their bodies is creation. Calling forth the gifts of others through management or supervision is creation. Dancing a dance, painting a portrait, sculpting a lifelike statue—each is creation.

Sharing Gifts

Living life as a Christian inevitably means the sharing of gifts through words and actions every day of the week, every week of the year. A thank-you, written or spoken, is a gift given and a gift received. Caring for a child or elderly parent is gift-giving. Making ethical decisions in the workplace is gift-giving. Child advocacy is a way to share one's gifts. Seeking justice in any part of God's world is gift-giving. Utilizing the gifts God has given us for a certain kind of work is gift-giving. The list goes on and on.

The Sunday liturgy highlights the sharing of gifts at the time of the offering. There we give money, almost always the result of the work of the people (the *liturgy* word again!). On the Sundays when the prayer of dedication acknowledges that the monetary gifts are gifts from the work of our hands, I am helped to connect my life with that Sunday's liturgy.

Ministry of Risk-Taking

Linking faith and daily life is risky business. When John, my late husband, was a member of the Evanston City Council, a church across the park from the ward he represented lobbied to open an all-night shelter for the homeless in its building. A carefully prepared proposal was presented to the council one Monday night and scheduled to be presented for vote two weeks later. On Tuesday, the hand-delivered letters of protest began to appear in our mailbox. "Having those people in our neighborhood will endanger the lives of our children, lower property values, increase crime," our neighbors wrote. Messages of protest were left on the answering machine. The "Letters to the Editor" section of the local weekly newspaper expressed similar, though more tactfully worded, messages—occasionally unsigned.

The other alderman from our ward unenthusiastically committed himself to a negative vote. Long-time friends promised to withdraw support in the next election if John supported the proposal. A handful of letters and messages urged John to vote yes.

He responded to every message and letter, explaining to each protester why he would support the proposal. The shelter was designed to protect lives and property, not endanger them. The homeless were in far greater danger from the weather, serious illness, and other perils than were any of the citizens. Appropriate and sensitive safeguards would be taken. "How can we deny these less-fortunate people the chance for a warm and dry place to sleep?" he asked. The proposal passed because enough people were willing to take a risk. That's what ministry in daily life is all about.

Taking a tough stand against discriminatory hiring practices, befriending a worker who has been treated unfairly, speaking out for a candidate whose platform of inclusion you support, advocating for children, seeking accessibility

WORSHIP&
DAILY
L I F E

for participants with disabilities, or lobbying for environmental controls means taking a risk. Many individuals and families know from experience that these kinds of risks often lead to alienation from family or coworkers.

The Church—Called to Make the Connection

If laypeople are to take seriously the ways in which their daily lives offer opportunities for ministry, the gap between their faith and their daily lives must be closed. The church, the chief proponent of the faith, has responsibility for disciple-making.

Just as Jesus called only a few apart to serve as his right-hand disciples, so does the church. Some, according to the writer of Ephesians, are given gifts to be "apostles, some prophets, some evangelists, some pastors and teachers" (Ephesians 4:11). Whatever their gifts, wherever their calling, the role of clergy and church professionals is singular— "to equip the saints for the work of ministry" (Ephesians 4:12). Contemporary authors such as Verna Dozier, Richard Broholm, William Diehl, and Anne Rowthorn concur. If the laity are ever to take seriously their responsibility for serving the world through their everyday lives, it will happen because the church has taken seriously its role as "equipping center," a phrase coined by Diehl, a Lutheran layman. It is virtually impossible for Christians to understand any connection between their daily lives and worship, without assistance from within the faith community.

Increased emphasis on the Covenant of Baptism is the place to begin. The people in the pew need assistance in understanding that it is baptism, not ordination, that makes us all the people of God and calls us to ministry. Adult candidates for baptism are asked if they will promise to be faithful to the church and to be Christ's representatives in the world. Being Christ's representatives in the world *is* being faithful to the mission of the church. It is also being faithful to the God we worship and the Christ whose name every Christian bears. These questions from the Baptismal Covenant imply that life and liturgy are inextricably linked at the time of baptism. The only credential Christians need for doing ministry, for being Christ's representatives in the world, is the Certificate of Baptism. It should hang on our office walls, above diplomas and other certifying documents. Baptism is a central sacramental act in the life of the worshiping community. Living sacramentally in one's daily life is the result.

During a Lenten adult study series on spirituality and work, one member of the class reported on his reading of a small booklet for lawyers in the series entitled *The Spirituality of Work.*

He was beginning to see the sacramental aspect of his work, especially when he was able to restore justice to an otherwise unjust situation. Another lawyer chimed in with her agreement. "If I pay attention, I'll find the sacramental aspects of the work I do," she said, astonished that she could even use *sacramental* and *work* in the same sentence!

To connect work and worship, or life and liturgy, or ministry and daily life requires an inevitable blurring of the lines ordinarily separating the sacred and the secular. To keep them separate is to create a dichotomy that, in reality, doesn't exist. Human beings are created as whole people. We wear the shoes of everyday life into the house of worship and out again into the world.

Equipping laity for ministry in the world means bringing our whole lives to the act of worship. Wearing our work shoes and clothes to worship is one way to do that. In soccer season, several of the children in our congregation arrive at worship on Sunday wearing their soccer uniforms in order to facilitate getting to their afternoon games on time. They do it for this practical reason, but these children have the right idea. Whether they are aware of it or not, they link their daily lives to their faith lives in a very visible way. They go from worship to an "everyday" place of their lives, a place that re-creates their bodies and spirits. How appropriate that they first wear their team's colors to the place where lessons of the faith are taught and learned!

Placing the tools or symbols of people's daily lives on the altar every Sunday is another way to help us connect faith and daily life. Involve laity in study of the lectionary, which indirectly involves them in sermon preparation. Use laity-written prayers, litanies, calls to worship, affirmations, and prayers of confessions. Provide study that helps laity translate the biblical story into their own stories.

Christians will transform their workplaces, homes, communities, neighborhoods, and the global community when they are equipped with the tools and support they need to do it— when the church takes more seriously the "holy" of their everyday lives. The people of God will find new meaning for their lives. When Sunday liturgies truly become "the work of the people," they will look vastly different than they presently look in most churches.

Progress in United Methodism

Within the last twelve to sixteen years The United Methodist Church, primarily in response to the efforts of laypeople, has begun to take more seriously the ministry of the laity—in the church, at least. In 1988, General Conference

WORSHIP&
DAILY
LIFE

adopted a resolution calling for the term *minister* to be used in *The Book of Discipline of The United Methodist Church* when referring to the whole people of God, and the terms *pastor, ordained minister,* or *diaconal minister* when referring to ordained or consecrated people. That same year, General Conference stretched its understanding when it listed as the first responsibility of the local church lay leader "fostering awareness of the role of laity both within the congregation and through their ministries in the home, work place, community, and world and finding ways within the community of faith to recognize all these ministries." (From *The Book of Discipline of The United Methodist Church—1988,* ¶251.1, page 145. Copyright © 1988 by The United Methodist Publishing House. Used by permission.)

In 1992, in further recognition of the gifts of the laity, General Conference voted to add laypeople to the membership of the Conference Board of Ordained Ministry and agreed in 1996 to give those lay members the vote on all matters. Still, these consciousness-raising efforts have focused primarily on the ministry of the laity within the church.

More recent efforts by the General Board of Higher Education and Ministry, through its then Division of Diaconal Ministry, moved the general church beyond the walls of the church building when it sponsored a consultation in April of 1993 on liturgy and work. Laypeople, diaconal ministers, and clergy from across the country were invited to present papers and reflections on the connection of worship and work. The consultation raised a number of issues about both work and worship that the whole church needs to deal with, and provided the church significant learnings on the subject. At the very least, this consultation provided thought-provoking consciousness-raising on the subject. A summary of the issues raised by the consultation was later recorded in a booklet entitled *The Unity of Liturgy and Life: A Study of the Relationship Between Worship and Work,* published in 1995. Many of the ideas explained in this chapter were presented during that consultation.

Worship and Daily Life: A Resource for Worship Planners

The congregation needs and is asking for resources that will help them connect their faith and their daily lives in concrete ways. The General Board of Discipleship is attempting to respond. This volume is intended to heighten the church's awareness of the connection of life and liturgy and provide "Monday" liturgies for the church to use on Sunday. I applaud this effort.

The liturgies that follow are truly "the work of the people." You will find here greetings, prayers of petition, litanies, prayers of confession, affirmations of faith, prayers of dedication, prayers of thanksgiving and intercession, prayers for opening meetings, prayers for sending forth, and suggestions for creating meaningful worship settings. They are the result of a two-day writing conference held in February 1998.

Our writing was guided by a number of principles and statements that emerged as we wrote. I share them here:

1. relevance to the everyday world;
2. turning points and meaningful moments in daily life;
3. theological significance of the insignificant (holiness of the ordinary);
4. an expectation of the presence of God—acknowledging God's presence;
5. centrality of the Baptismal Covenant as basis for ministry in daily life;
6. being theological without using archaic, misunderstood theological language;
7. making sure that what is written can be understood by everyone;
8. accessibility to God—tools become accessible to a large number of people;
9. recognition of cultural diversity;
10. God calls each of us, and wherever we are called, God strengthens us;
11. push toward concreteness of language;
12. simplicity of language and awareness of nuances that elevate it;
13. teaching that God is in "work" places;
14. inclusive language;
15. joy of the journey;
16. The goal is transformation.

Following the chapters of written witnesses, you will find additional resources that are designed to assist you in planning the Sunday liturgy—resources that are ecumenical, inter-religious, and inter-ethnic in nature. The General Board of Discipleship has every hope that the resources presented here will provide new lenses to look at the "people's work."

Connecting Liturgy and Life

A second image is offered by the Center for the Ministry of the Laity—a picture of wholeness. In this image, the stick figure is replaced by a full person who appears in the center, comprised of dozens of smaller figures of all colors and sizes. Each arm and foot of this person is placed firmly in the places of everyday life—the government building, the school, the home, the factory, the high-rise, the neighborhood. In the core

WORSHIP& DAILY LIFE

of the person are the font and table.

The whole church is called to be the people of God in the world. We are called to embody the living Christ in the everyday places of our lives—with family, neighbors, coworkers—and to make a difference in all the arenas of life. Let it be so!

Greetings

Wherever God's people gather, whether in corporate worship, small-group ministries, workplace gatherings, family dinners, or church meetings, God is present. In whatever settings these greetings are used, they call us to remember and claim God's life-giving love, present in our midst.

COME! Come and be present in this place.
Come, bring your body, mind, and spirit
 to be present in (*name of community, place of worship, room, and so forth*).
Listen to the sounds around you,
 to the people gathering,
 to the sighs and longings of their hearts.
Listen to the words being said,
 to unspoken questions
 asking if this is a place where people are heard.
Listen to the words of welcome,
 to the gracious invitation to worship (*to participate, to learn*).
Look at the signs of gathering,
 at the open spaces filled with color and light,
 at the sanctuary prepared for worship,
 (*at the seats and tables that are set for work*).
Look for the signs of hope to be fulfilled.
Know that this gathering is a gift
 where God's presence can meet you,
 where all long for moments of grace.
Remember that Christ promised to be present
 whenever we are gathered in his name. **Amen.**

WORSHIP& DAILY LIFE

Leader: Good morning, you chosen ones of God.
People: Good morning.
Leader: God calls you to accept God's blessings for your life.
People: Today we accept God's blessing to experience the peace, joy, and love that passes human understanding.

Welcome to this haven,
   this place of hospitality.
Here the God of the still small voice
   waits with eternal patience
   for us to endure the whirlwind,
   the fire, and the earthquake.
Welcome to this resting place,
   where angels bring refreshment.
Whether you wake or sleep, walk or run,
   speak or enter the divine silence,
   know that God beckons us
   to enter this time, this place.

From the highway and from the skies,
   from the office and from the streets,
   from the jail and from the classroom,
   from the kitchen and from the garage,
   from the bank and from the gym,
   from the table and from the font
   a voice beckons.
May we hear and may we follow.

Leader: Good morning, ye chosen ones of God.
People: Good morning.
Leader: In the hustle and bustle of life, God calls us to be still and experience God.
People: The Lord is our strength and our refuge. We wait upon the Lord and our strength is renewed.

Welcome to this place.
This is the place of your baptism,
 your call to ministry.
We are glad you are here.
May the blessings of the risen Christ be abundant
 today and throughout your week,
 wherever you are.

Greetings in the name of Jesus Christ. Bring all you are to this place. Bring your sorrows, your burdens, your strengths and needs. This is a place where you will find strength and support. Greetings in the name of Jesus Christ.

Greetings to all of you in the name of Jesus Christ. You have come from different places and have left behind people and places dear to you. You are welcome to this place. May our time together be a time of spiritual growth, a time of reflection, so that you may return to ministries with friends and families renewed in your understanding of who you are and who goes with you.

Welcome to this faith community. Welcome to this time of worship and reflection. You bring all the places of your daily lives with you. As you are blessed by the work you do, the relationships you have, and the locations where you spend your time, may you be blessed in this time and place. The grace and mercy of God, Christ, and the Holy Spirit be with you all. **Amen.**

In some places the wind blows all the time.
It whips coattails around and rearranges hairdos.
The wind is a source of power.
May the winds of God's Spirit transform us today.

WORSHIP & DAILY LIFE

Leader: Welcome to the church of Jesus Christ!

People: We come from different cultures and races.

Leader: All are invited into the doors of our sanctuary.

People: We are adults, children, and youth.

Leader: All are invited to the altar of our church.

People: We are women, men, girls, and boys.

Leader: All are invited to the table for Communion.

**People: We are employed, unemployed, with limited
income, and with great wealth.**

Leader: All are invited to the baptismal font.

People: We experience God in many ways.

Leader: All are invited to share with us in fellowship.

People: We come, Lord, we come.

Leader: Welcome, all of you!

Grace to you and peace,
   my sisters, my brothers,
   who are engaged in life and stretched,
   at times confused.

Grace to you and peace,
   my brothers, my sisters,
   who are bewildered and delighted
   with what life brings,
   heartened by the stories
   of those who love you well,
   those you seek to love—
   a prisoner, a child, a homeless one,
   a sibling, a spouse.

Grace to you,
   restless to be still, to be quiet,
   to live beside a silent candle
   in the urgent, swirling air.

Grace to you, and peace.

Greetings in the name of Jesus Christ.

Our lives are varied, but we share a common core in Christian ministry. That core, in whatever specifics we engage in daily, is the heart and soul of our lives. For many our lives are like a whirlwind, a hurricane of activities and coordination; yet there is a center that provides a sense of peace and calm. That center is in God in Jesus Christ. It is the common denominator that brings us together and grounds our ministry. Thanks be to God.

You come bringing gifts,
not *in* your hands
but your hands themselves.
In your eyes and your voice,
your face and your spirit.

They speak of you.
They say, "Here are all the places I have been.
Here are the people I have known.
Here is my spirit, not tucked away
but worn as a treasured garment."

You say, "Here is my gift.
It is the best I have.
I bring myself,
knowing that when we leave,
because of your gift
I will look a little more like you
and a little more like God."

Frantic busyness,
   Takes over the pace of our day.
      Center us, O God.

Thanksgiving & Praise

In The Great Thanksgiving for Advent we claim,

> *It is right, and a good and joyful thing,*
> *always and everywhere to give thanks to you,*
> *almighty God, creator of heaven and earth.*

The following prayers and litanies remind us that "always and everywhere" includes the workplace, the schoolroom, the home, and the highways.

God of the seed and the soil, the seasons and the weather, we bless you for the seed of your holy work among us, bringing new generations of service and love to fruition. You promise to be with us in all times and all places, you bid us to hear your voice in the journey of every day. We thank you that your loving eyes behold us in all the places you have scattered us, hallowing the hospital and the classroom, the construction site and the courtroom, the sanctuary and the jail, the farm and the supermarket, the skies and the seas, the bank and the concert hall, the projects and the subdivisions, the streets and the meadows.

Let us celebrate your divine eyes seeing us; let us see all that you hope for in us. We thank you for the soil of our hearts and the garden of our place on this earth, for the growth of your love in a multitude of blooms, for the seasons of ripening that yield your goodness in the face of all dying and rising, through all seasons and weather, by the grace of Jesus Christ, rising again among us all. **Amen.**

WORSHIP&
DAILY
LIFE

Leader: What thanksgivings do we bring before God this day?

People: We bring thanksgivings of our hearts—
for the joy of a small child discovering a flower,
for the tender touch of an encouraging hand,
for love extended without expectation.

All: **O Spirit of God, you give us moments that only our**
hearts can hold—moments of warmth and awareness
when our souls sing. Thank you, God, for nourishing
relationships on this incredible journey of life. May
your name be praised!

Leader: What thanksgivings do we bring before God this day?

People: We bring thanksgivings of our minds—
for learning that has come through the experience,
for print and pictures that stimulate us to inquire
and know more of your world,
for those who teach us in formal and informal ways,
freely sharing their knowledge and understandings.

All: **O God of Wisdom, you instill in us the desire to know**
and understand. Thank you for giving us minds that
can seek and learn. We thank you for those who teach
and help our minds grow. May your name be praised!

Leader: What thanksgivings do we bring before God this day?

People: We bring thanksgivings of our physical world—
for strength to do our daily work,
for eyes and ears that are doorways to your creation,
for water and food to support life.

All: **O God of all Creation, you provide for our daily needs**
in countless ways. Thank you, God, for all that sustains
life. May your name be praised!

Leader: We offer these thanksgivings in praise and gratitude,
O loving God. Amen.

O God, who art all-powerful and all-knowing, who knows
where we have come from and where we are going even
though we do not know these things about ourselves, we
thank you that you are God all by yourself, and that there is
no problem so big that you cannot handle.

Therefore, God, we thank you for the opportunity to bring
to you the concerns of our hearts, knowing that you can and
will solve them in a way that exceeds our meager understanding or expectation. In the name of Jesus the Christ we
pray. **Amen.**

Note: You may want to print only the first and last sentences of the following leader's section, leaving points of ellipsis between.

Leader: Our week has been filled with schedules to meet, responsibilities to uphold, and people who demand from us. We find ourselves tired, frustrated, and stressed. So in this place of worship let us spend some time quietly in the presence of God. Close your eyes. Take a few deep breaths. As you enter this time of prayer, release your concerns to God and think on these things. Picture yourself sitting by a wooded stream and putting your bare feet into the cool, babbling water (*pause*); relaxing in a porch swing on a moonlit evening and listening to the sound of katydids (*pause*); walking in a cool and fragrant garden on an early morning (*pause*); rocking in the arms of a loving parent who gently rubs your back while humming a quiet song to you (*long pause*). Let us speak together these words:

All: **O God, thank you for the quiet moments that bring us back into an awareness of your presence and your love. May such moments renew us and refresh us. Help us take from them the energy we need to work and serve as your people in this world. Amen.**

Awaken today,
  eyes open, blood pumping fast.
To all, life is gift.

Lord, in the quietness of the hour we come to you, thanking you for the sunshine. As the rays fall brilliantly across our faces and we feel their warmth, our hearts are warmed by the assurance that you are ever present as we seek to establish an even stronger relationship with you. Lord, thank you for all of creation. Thank you for the birds and their melodious songs, for the squirrels that greet us in their own special ways, and for the chipmunk who wants to play hide-and-go-seek. In all of these, Lord, we see the fingertip of your handiwork, and for this we are most grateful. Thank you, Lord, for allowing us again to become refreshed in thee. **Amen.**

Thank you, God,
for peanut butter and jelly,
macaroni and cheese,
Toostie Roll Pops and pizza,
spaghetti and long bread sticks,
chicken legs and corn on the cob,
sweet cereal with cold milk,
and everything we like to taste.

Thank you, God,
for new flannel pajamas,
socks with no holes in them,
shoes with Velcro,
T-shirts,
deep pockets,
Scout uniforms,
school colors,
and everything we like to wear.

Thank you, God,
for bikes and roller blades,
swimming pools and soccer fields,
for trees to climb up
and hills to roll down,
for clubhouses and hiding places,
and everywhere we like to play.

Thank you, God,
for crayons and pencils,
work sheets and quizzes,
spelling words and flash cards,
computers and library books,
teachers and librarians,
and everything that helps us learn.

Thank you, God,
for parents and neighbors,
grandmas and grandpas,
sisters and brothers,
teammates and partners,
stuffed animals and real live pets,
and everyone who cares for us.

Thank you, God,
for everything.
Amen.

This day, O loving God, is a gift that we accept with joy-filled hearts. Who could have brought us to this time except a God who wishes us abundance? You are a God of surprises, for we did not believe that this (*birth, wedding, graduation, or other occasion*) would bring such awareness of your guiding hand. Your love surrounds us and your light is shining through all who are gathered here.

Thank you, God, for the many wonderful blessings of this day. **Amen.**

Almighty and merciful God, thanks for your amazing grace. We are grateful that we can never sink so low that your grace and mercy does not come looking for us. Thank you for extending your love to us even before we were formed in our mama's womb. You called us and allowed your Holy Spirit to infiltrate us. For this, O God, we are most grateful. Thank you, Lord, for a mind stayed on thee. Our hearts are happy all the day long. **Amen.**

Lord, we come at this time to thank you for the many blessings that you have bestowed upon us. We thank you that we were able to rise this morning, still clothed in our right mind; that we were able to go into the kitchen and find food to eat, able to go to the closet and choose clothes to wear. We thank you, Lord, for a reasonable portion of health, significant work to do, a family to love, a neighborhood where we share one another's concerns, a church that reaches out to the needy, and, most of all, for your darling Son, Jesus, who died that we might have the right to eternal life. Lord, never let us take these things for granted. We know that a grateful heart is a happy heart. In Jesus' name we pray. **Amen.**

Thank you, God, for friends and food,
for teachers and shelter,
for leaders and warm clothing,
for healers and medicines,
for protectors and safe places,
for advocates and fresh air,
for family and clean water. **Amen.**

WORSHIP & DAILY LIFE

Leader: Today we thank the Lord for being the source of life and giving the gift of life.
People: This is the day that the Lord has made.
Leader: We, along with all life on earth, have been given this great gift.
People: This is the day that the Lord has made.
Leader: We thank you today for just being. We thank you for eyes that see, ears that hear, hands that touch.
People: This is the day that the Lord has made.
Leader: Let us never take this great gift of life for granted. Let us not take it for granted on this day!
People: This is the day that the Lord has made.
Leader: Let us rejoice and be glad in it!
All: Amen.

Most merciful God,
We give thanks for the work you give us to do.
   Our work gives us a sense of importance.
We give thanks for the people we encounter daily.
   People give us a sense of belonging.
We give thanks for schedules and routines.
   They help us to feel grounded in a changing world.
We give thanks for Jesus Christ.
   Christ's love gives meaning to all of life.
Amen.

Great God of the day and of the night, we speak our gratitude for your dream of us and for the fruition of your dreams in us. You guide us in the night and by day, a pillar of fire and a pillar of cloud, weaving in us a sturdy web of future and memory. We praise you for the ways you meet us, both sleeping and waking, working and resting, before and behind us. Thank you, thank you, thank you. **Amen.**

From the earth springs the oak,
   from the sky fall the rains,
      from our work comes its fruit,
         and from our hearts, your praise.

O God, your presence in daily life is a delight!
You give us eyes to see holy moments in ordinary things:
   in the bustle of getting children to soccer practice;
   in the hallway conversation with a colleague whose
      daughter has stage four cancer;
   on the phone when we ask an aging parent, "How are you
      today?"
   in the traffic jam when you prompt us to make room
      for a merging car.
Thank you for not allowing us to devalue small things!
Thank you for giving eyes to see that life is made up of small
   things, and for allowing grace to merge into the stream of
   eating, bathing, working, touching, and resting.
Thank you for your presence in every moment of our lives.
Amen.

Gracious Creator, giver of all life, we thank you today for the gift of simply being. How often we take our lives for granted, and yet there you are to provide the very foundation of our waking and acting. We pour out our thanksgiving for this gift. We realize that nothing is guaranteed in life, least of all our lives. How wonderful and amazing is the gift of life. May the living of this day be a reflection of our thanksgiving. May our blessing infuse all we do and say on this day. May we be moved to lead our lives as a reflection of this great gift. **Amen.**

Thank you, Lord, for unshakable inner security that comes only from your powerful presence in our lives. As our spirits meet with yours, may we have holiness of heart and life. Lord, thank you for giving your darling Son, Jesus the Christ, to fill us in all places where we are empty.

Thank you for this gift that touches our lives and calls us to climb the spiritual tree and enjoy the fruits yielded by a life grounded in you. We are rescued from perishing when we eat from this tree of life. We no longer thirst when we drink from this everflowing stream. Jesus saves. **Amen.**

**WORSHIP&
DAILY
LIFE**

O great God of heaven and earth, we thank you
　for the nurseries made ready for our little ones,
　and for your star nurseries of cosmic dust and new planets.
We thank you
　for the miracle of growing that works in each child,
　and for the growth of new forests over clear-cut fields.
We thank you
　for the development of each boy and girl,
　and for the transformation of rain into rivers.
We thank you
　for the young adults who generate new leadership,
　and for the breath of clean air after a storm.
We thank you
　for the process of maturation that deepens wisdom,
　and for the still water and haven of wetlands.
We thank you
　for the course of aging that clarifies lasting values,
　and for the perspective of mountain heights.
O great God of heaven and earth,
　of babies and of great-grandparents,
　we offer you grateful hearts, stretched by all you give
　within us, among us, and beyond us,
　from cells to constellations. **Amen.**

O Lord, giver of all life, we are thankful today for a day of sabbath. We are thankful for the opportunity to worship you. We come from a busy week of tending families, teaching children, working productively, juggling roles, assuming responsibilities, and carrying out our assigned tasks. We are thankful for the gift of energy and time in the meeting of our responsibilities.

However, we are also thankful for a respite from our work. We are thankful for this day of sabbath, on which we can concentrate our gratitude in worship of you. May we extend this sabbath during our work week. Enable us to stop and pause in thanksgiving each day this coming week, offering to you the praise and thanks you deserve. Through your child, Jesus Christ. **Amen.**

God of every goodness,
We give you thanks for all that gives life its savor:
  for work done well, and rest;
  for good food, and strength we draw from it;
  for familiar things, and new;
  for the spring of youth, and age's season;
  for the touch of loved ones, and the kindness of strangers;
  for times of gathering with your people in prayer,
  and the prayer we carry into work, school, and home;
  for the spoken word, and silence.
God of every, every goodness,
hear our thanks. **Amen.**

God, you wired us with wonder and delight.
The world and life are so amazing that we cannot help being
  learners and students.
We thank you for the compelling urge to know and to grow.
We thank you for nursery school teachers welcoming chil-
  dren we parents can hardly bear to let out of our sight.
We thank you for teachers and school staff planning and
  preparing classes.
We thank you for high school students searching for accep-
  tance and struggling with math and history.
We thank you for college faculty opening up the world to
  those seeking knowledge.
We thank you for researchers and graduate students exploring
  the frontiers of service to the human family.
We praise you for teachers and students living as disciples of
  Jesus in the halls and classroom, on the basketball court
  and at the dance.
We praise you for librarians organizing books and computer
  links so that we can interact with ideas and people we may
  never meet face to face.
We praise you for teachers caring compassionately for those
  who are falling behind because something is wrong at
  home or in the heart.
God, you wired us with wonder and delight. The world and
  life are so amazing that we cannot help being learners and
  students. **Amen.**

Thank you, God, for those who, like you,
  repair our homes and our hearts:
    for electricians who fix our wiring and restore power lines;
    for surgeons who repair blocked arteries and remove tumors;
    for plumbers who unclog drains and fix leaking pipes;
    for therapists who dispel the demons of our mind.

Thank you, God, for those who, like your Son,
  teach and guide us:
    for teachers who give our children knowledge;
    for saints who have taught us the true meaning of faith;
    for professors who have challenged and pushed us to think;
    for dads and moms who teach us to be uncommonly wise.

Thank you, God, for those who, like your Word,
  enrich our lives in the arts:
    for singers whose voices make our hearts soar;
    for writers whose written word gives us a new perspective;
    for musicians who help us hear God's songs;
    for painters whose images give us a new vision.

Thank you, God, for those who, like your Spirit,
  work behind the scenes and out of the spotlight:
    for secretaries who by their work make our work better;
    for janitors who clean up after us;
    for medical clerks who keep track of our records;
    for cooks who make our meals.

We thank you, God, for all the ways in which
  the work we do imitates the work you do.
We pray that in our work we glorify you.
We pray that through our work we may reveal you.
We pray that as we work we may be aware of working with
  you. **Amen.**

Leader: Oh, what a beautiful morning!

People: I see the presence of the Lord.

Leader: Even in my trials,

People: I feel the presence of the Lord.

Leader: In all things give thanks.

People: This is the will of the Lord.

Leader: The world is filled with people who are stressed.

People: Lord, be with us.

Leader: They spend their substance in riotous living, working to get things that they can't afford to impress folk that they don't even like.

People: Lord, be with us.

Leader: God sent his Son, the perfect gift, to die on the cross, be buried, and rise again.

People: Thank you, God, for an avenue to find true fulfillment that can never be found in things.

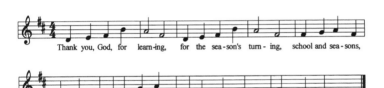

Confessions

Many of these confessions acknowledge that our actions in daily life and our words on Sunday morning are often not related. This reality is surely a cause for confession. Confession is a first step toward forgiveness and reconciliation. Through God's forgiveness we are able to start afresh, trying once again to be the disciples that God is calling us to be.

Here we are, Lord. We fold our hands in prayer and ask to know your presence in these moments. This has been a difficult week in many ways. We have longed for silence and a time to feel your comforting touch. Instead our days have been filled with noise, busyness, and stress.

We remember the things we thought should be done but did not do, the phone call or letter that might have helped someone know we care but that we did not send. We remember wanting to give a touch of encouragement but holding back, fearing that it would not be accepted; the excellence we hoped from the work of our hands, but that we compromised because of distractions and haste.

These hands of ours so often do not do your work in our homes or workplaces. Instead they busily respond to the pressures around them, and feel weary in doing. As we fold our hands in prayer, we know, Lord, that this is not the way we wish to live or what you intend for us. We wish to be inspired by your presence. We want our hands to become instruments of service in your name. We want to touch others with your love.

Help us in the coming days to seek your direction in the use of our time and abilities. Guide our hands to be instruments of your will. We ask for your presence to lead us. Be with us, O Lord. **Amen.**

When we measure our worth
  by the number of hours we spend at our desks,
    forgive us, Lord.
When we fail to notice that the snow has melted
  and the trees are beginning to bud,
    forgive us, Lord.
When finishing one more project is more important
  than comforting a hurting friend,
    forgive us, Lord.
When the calendar guides our lives
  more than Scripture does,
    forgive us, Lord.
When we proclaim that grace is free to all
  and then act as if we must earn our salvation,
    forgive us, Lord.

Leader: Holy God, holy and mighty, we confess the smallness of our vision.
People: God so loved the world.
Leader: You, Lord, are making all things new and preparing a new heaven and a new earth, while we behave as if the church is all you care about.
People: God so loved the world.
Leader: You are at work in every place of human suffering and need, while we hold meetings wondering how we can get more people to come to church.
People: God so loved the world.
Leader: You, Lord, are looking for every man and woman, child and young person, to co-labor with you in finishing your creation, while we persist in wanting to make church members.
People: God so loved the world.
Leader: Heal us and help us to see what you see.
People: Heal us and help us, Lord.
Leader: Heal us and help us to see where you are working at operating tables, auto repair shops, hair salons, and recording studios.
People: Heal us and help us, Lord.
Leader: Heal us and help us to see that you are already working where we work and live.
All: **Heal us and help us, Lord.**
        Heal us and help us to be disciples
        and to make disciples.
        Heal us and help us, Lord.

Lord, we are guilty about a lot of things we think you say
are bad.
The truth is, we don't even see the things that make you
mad and sad.
Our hearts condemn us when we say a four-letter word, yet
we don't even realize that our pent-up anger is toxic to
our children and our workplace.
Our hearts condemn us when we don't take time for devo-
tional reading, while we ignore the hurt on a colleague's
face.
Our hearts condemn us when we skip church to go to a ball
game, while we ignore the homeless and the rundown
neighborhood we drive through on the way to work each
day.
For all that we don't see in our daily life, forgive us.
Give us new eyes to see what you see and new hands to
work where you are working through Jesus Christ our
Lord. **Amen.**

God of unconditional love and grace, we confess that we
have often believed that by our work we could become
your beloved children. Remind us that you have loved us
before and will love us after all we may do or be.

We confess that we have often excluded ourselves from your
beloved family because of the kind of work that we may do.
Remind us that in your great love for us in Jesus Christ,
there is nothing that can separate us from your love.

We confess that we have often excluded ourselves from
your beloved family because we believe we are too young,
too old, unable, or unprepared to make a significant contri-
bution. Remind us of how Jesus welcomed the little ones,
touched the isolated ones, and healed the hurting ones;
remind us now of his welcome for every one of us.

God of unconditional love and grace, may we grow to
accept your mercy and forgiveness so that through us your
mercy and forgiveness may flow to all we meet. In Jesus'
name. **Amen.**

Note: The worship leader begins reading 1 John 4:7-13 (NRSV) aloud. As the leader reads the passage, each person in the congregation chooses one of the laments and begins reading it aloud in a soft voice, with everyone reading their chosen laments simultaneously. As they read, they should gradually get louder until they come to the line, "Silence my frenzy, O God, and let me hear your voice," which should be said in a soft, prayerful voice. The leader should pace his or her speed of reading so that verse 13 is read immediately after the laments are finished. Another way to use this confession is for the leader to read 1 John 4:7-13, and then for different sections of the congregation to read the laments in order rather than all at the same time.

Leader: "Beloved, let us love one another, because love is from God; everyone who loves is born of God and knows God. . . ." (*Continue reading 1 John 4:7-13 while the congregation reads the laments.*)

Lament A: I couldn't sleep last night. After watching the news, my mind raced with images of a troubled world. What if I become unable to afford health care? What if I, or those I love, become the victim of violent crime? What if I make a mistake on my income tax return and owe more money than I have? It is frightening to think about such things. But I cannot keep from thinking about these things, though I tremble with fear when I do. Silence my frenzy, O God, and let me hear your voice.

Lament B: I am such a jerk. If people only knew the things I have done and the things I think about, they would probably not like me. I can remember actions from years past that still haunt me. I have hurt some people. Sometimes I feel ashamed even to pray. I am not the person I want to be. If people only knew the things I have done and the things I think about, they would probably not like me. Silence my frenzy, O God, and let me hear your voice.

Lament C: Where have I gone wrong? Why are the lives of people I love in such turmoil? Surely there is something I could have done to prevent it. If I only knew what that could be. I feel so powerless. I have many more questions than I have answers. Other people appear to be so confident, so gifted, always knowing the right thing to say. I feel like I am stumbling through life, always wondering where I have gone wrong. Silence my frenzy, O God, and let me hear your voice.

Lament D: There are some people I just can't stand. I don't understand the way they are, and I don't like being around them. They make me nervous. They cause problems. They hurt me. They are responsible for the terrible shape our country is in today. I would like to lock them all up, or send them all to some remote island where I will never have to deal with them again. They make my life difficult, and I am tired of putting up with them. There are some people I just can't stand. Silence my frenzy, O God, and let me hear your voice.

Leader: Lord, hear our heartfelt confessions today.
People: We have often shied away from talking about faith at our workplace.
Leader: We have worried that others would look down on us for such views.
People: We have kept a radical separation between our work life and our church life
Leader: As if we have been ashamed of our faith and calling.
People: Enable us, O Lord, to see that our faith and our work cannot be separated from each other.
Leader: Move us to share with boldness the good news of God's love for all. God has heard our confessions and forgives us lovingly.

We confess that often we only name your presence, living God, when we are in the church building. Forgive us, we pray, for the times and the places we fail to remember to turn to you, for the occasions when we forget or deny that we know you, you who are as close as our breathing and our own beating hearts.

Forgive us for all the conflicts in which we have neglected to claim your light and power to bring peace with justice. Forgive us when in our friendships your providence and purposes have gone unacknowledged. Forgive us for the meals we have shared that have gone ungraced by our gratitude for your bounty.

In joyful obedience, hold us, even as you release us from our past sins. Empower us for mending that which has been broken by our sinful action and inaction. Go before us to open new pathways of love in your daily companionship through Christ. **Amen.**

WORSHIP& DAILY LIFE

Almighty God, here we are again, telling you and those around us that we have failed to live up to all that we can be. We didn't listen very carefully to our friend yesterday. The birthday cards for friends and relatives are still lying on our desks, and some of those birthdays have already passed. We failed to call on our neighbor whose father died. These seem small omissions. If we serve you whenever we serve those around us, are we neglecting you as well? These are friends and family whose love and support we value. Waken us to the small opportunities in order that we may not neglect the large ones. Nudge us to find time to foster relationships with others, for in so doing we are caring for the relationship between you and us. **Amen.**

Merciful God,
We confess that we have often lived by our works
    rather than by faith in you.
When we have been offered a moment's quiet,
    we have crowded it with louder things.
When we have been given the presence
    of another person to enjoy,
      we have set forth an agenda for the time together.
When we have been called to delightful response,
    we have responded with resigned responsibility.
When we have seen grace dancing
    and known that we too might dance,
    we have instead worked harder.

Forgive us for believing a gospel of self-security
    rather than your gospel of complete provision.
Open us to the persistent prying of your loving kindness,
    that by the experience of your grace
    in our moments and days,
    we may come to know life
    as first a gift, then a task.
In the name of Jesus we pray. **Amen.**

Leader: We come today aware of our need for confession.

People: We confess today, O Lord, we have not taken your words in this service to heart.

Leader: We have spoken most of them by rote, hardly paying attention to their deeper meaning and relevance to our own individual lives.

People: We have participated in much of this service out of obligation rather than true feeling.

Leader: Shake us up, O Lord! Move us to see that we are active players in this service, not the audience who receive the blessings but the performers who give the blessing to you.

People: We ask for your forgiveness and the chance to change.

Leader: Now hear our personal and private prayers of confession.

(The people are asked to uplift personal and private prayers of confession in silence at this time.)

Leader: God forgives us and sets us free. We may live in the knowledge of this forgiveness.

People: We are freed to start anew and participate in this service from the depths of our hearts.

All: **Thanks be to God!**

Leader: We realize we have fallen short of your glory. Hear our prayers of confession.

People: We have heard your cry for justice, but we have used the excuse that we are only one voice amid many.

Leader: We have heard your cry for peace, but we have used the excuse that we need a strong military to protect our interests.

People: We have heard your cry for protecting the earth, but we have used the excuse that science will find a way to save our planet.

Leader: We have heard your cry for reconciliation with our brothers and sisters, but we have used the excuse that we do not know many of those who are of another race or culture.

People: We have heard your cry to help the poor and homeless, but we have used the excuse that they will misuse the help.

Leader: Lord, we have run out of simple excuses and now must face our own sinfulness. We are responsible for not acting on your cries, and we need to respond to your call for justice.

People: Forgive us, O Lord, and move us to action. Amen.

Affirmations of Faith

Sometimes our affirmations of faith sound like dry statements of theological concepts. The affirmations printed here are joyful affirmations of how God is working in our lives and in our world.

We believe in God, the Creator of this amazing universe, who continues to make all things new. From new galaxies to the birth of a child, from new learning and discoveries in science to the arrival of spring after a difficult winter, God is creating. We believe, O Creator God, that you are constantly weaving the fiber of goodness within the world.

We believe in Jesus Christ, the Savior of this world, who shows the way for living life to its full potential. It is Christ who leads us to seek forgiveness and conveys through his life and death the immense love of God available to all. It is Christ who asks us to have the hearts of little children and to trust and love God wholly and to love our neighbor as ourselves. We believe, O Christ, that you are constantly calling us to be transformed to your likeness.

Advent 2-99

We believe in the Holy Spirit, the presence of God daily in our lives, the Spirit of truth, justice, and love, who guides and informs us, and the comforting attendant who holds us when we are passing through dark valleys. Joy, patience, compassion—all come from the Holy Spirit. We believe, O Spirit of God, that you seek to be present in every dimension of our lives.

O triune God, may we know you fully and may our lives glorify you. **Amen.**

WORSHIP&
DAILY
LIFE

We believe that God is creating
  in the clay of a potter,
  in the music of an orchestra,
  in the bread of a baker.
We believe that Jesus Christ is present
  in the hospitality of a waitress,
  in the care of a social worker,
  in the voice of a teacher.
We believe that the Holy Spirit is moving
  in the healing touch of a doctor,
  in the actions of a peacemaker,
  in the laughter of a child.

Leader: Alarm clocks, toasters, bathroom mirrors, zippers,
shoelaces, a good-bye kiss, and the day begins.

People: God is with us in our rising.

Leader: Time clocks, sticky notes, phone calls, coffee break,
colleagues, scheduling, preparing, supervising,
listening, and our workday unfolds.

People: God is with us as we work.

Leader: Grocery lists, dustpans, lawn mowers, oven mitts,
pillowcases, laundry baskets, kitty litter, pliers, and
our houses are maintained.

People: God is with us in our homes.

Leader: Embraces, instructions, sticker charts, bibs, checkup
calls, apologies, private jokes, quiet talks, and our
relationships continue.

People: God is with us in our families.

Leader: Hot plates, salt shakers, crumbs, forks, big bites, sips,
toothpicks, and we receive our meals.

People: God is with us when we eat.

Leader: News reports, bathrobes, locking doors, another
chapter, night-lights, tomorrow's list, and another day
is over.

People: God is with us through the night.

All: At every moment of our life, God is with us.
Alleluia! Alleluia!

We believe that every infinitesimal act of kindness is enhanced by God's infinite power and eternal love.

We believe that all people are of irreplaceable value in God's economy.

We believe that underemployed people and unemployed people and even unemployable people are of sacred worth and have vital jobs in the building of God's dreams.

We believe that every worker and job bears within them the signs of God's own presence: the waitress who serves us dinner, the firefighter who rescues us, the doctor who repairs our wounds, the homeless man who redeems our cans. God is made visible through the work of the people.

We believe that we are called by God to be workers for God. Each of us has gifts for ministry. Each of us has been given opportunities through which we can make God known.

2/6/00

We believe in God, Creator of all people and places. God is present everywhere, making the ordinary places of our lives holy. When humanity hurts, God is there. When the people of the earth rejoice, God is there.

We believe in Jesus Christ, Son of God and son of Mary. Jesus walked this earth, healing the sick, talking to the stranger, speaking the truth in love, and risking his life for what he believed. He risked speaking out on behalf of those who could not speak for themselves. He continues to walk with us.

2/4/01

We believe in the Holy Spirit, holy mystery and wholly mysterious, who pushes us into places where we did not plan to go. The Holy Spirit is the sign of God in our lives.

We believe that God has given us gifts to be used in God's ongoing creation. We are called by God in baptism to go beyond ourselves, to reach out to others, to advocate for the helpless and homeless and marginalized, wherever we are.

WORSHIP& DAILY LIFE

We believe there is no place where God cannot be found.
　　On street corners and in dark alleys,
　　　　God is there.
　　In hospital rooms and in hospice centers,
　　　　God is there.
　　In factories and in taco stands,
　　　　God is there.
　　In classrooms and in kitchens,
　　　　God is there.
　　In prisons and in amusement parks,
　　　　God is there.
　　In daycare centers and in homeless shelters,
　　　　God is there.
　　In churches and in boot camps,
　　　　God is there.
　　In playgrounds and in mortuaries,
　　　　God is there.
　　In bars and in board rooms,
　　　　God is there.
　　In grocery stores and in mall shops,
　　　　God is there.
God is with us.
God is with us where we live.
God is with us where we work.
God is with us.

Petitions

These prayers of petition call upon God to act on our behalf in all places and situations of our lives. Although these prayers are appropriate for many settings and situations, the italic headings suggest specific times for which, or people for whom, these prayers may be particularly meaningful.

(*For meetings*)

Leader: Speak to us, O God, as we carefully ponder the decisions before us.

People: Help us listen for your voice among us, O God.

Leader: Listen to our hearts and remove distrust and anxiety among us.

People: Help us trust in your presence with us, O God.

Leader: Help us use wisely the information we have to make the needed decisions.

People: Help us learn what is important in your sight, O God.

Leader: Help us value each person's ideas, information, and feelings.

People: Help us love one another, O God.

Leader: Teach us how to decide in light of your will.

People: Help us seek the greater good for all, O God.

Leader: We pray this prayer in the name of your Son, Jesus Christ. **Amen.**

WORSHIP & DAILY LIFE

(For meetings)

God, we are here to conduct a meeting about the business of your church. As we converse, let our deliberations lead to the accomplishment of your purpose. Help each of us put aside our personal agendas and let a spirit of unity prevail. Open our minds to see your mission of love and service. Open our eyes that we may see the needs in the world. Guide us in the path that we should follow to accomplish your purpose. In Jesus' name we pray. **Amen.**

(For meetings)

Gracious God, you have called us from the busyness of our lives to this place. This is your time and place. You are here. May this be a time of thoughtful deliberation, healthy discussion, and careful discernment. May all that we say be acceptable in your sight. And may our decisions reflect an understanding that we live by your grace. Help us feel your presence with us. **Amen.**

(For meetings)

For the decisions before us, Lord,
    make plain your way.
For the actions our decisions require,
    grant us courage and resolve.
For those touched by the decisions we make,
    fill us with compassion and guide us with your wisdom,
In the name of Jesus Christ, in whom we live, lead, and pray. **Amen.**

(For meetings)

O God, who has manifested your love among the poor, may we all realize that we are among the deprived in direct proportion to our lack of love, our lack of forgiveness, and our failure to be faithful to the call you have placed on our lives. Lord, thank you for calling imperfect people to work in imperfect situations. Recognizing our imperfections as we undertake this ministry, we rely on you, Lord, to guide both the plans and the programs. Let each decision that we implement be guided by you, that the work now before us will not be done in vain. In Jesus' name we pray. **Amen.**

(*At the time of a death*)

We bring our burdened and grieving hearts to you, O God. We feel our loss overwhelming us, and we search our questioning minds to understand the mysteries of life and death. (*Name*) was a precious part of our lives, and we feel we have lost part of ourselves in (*his/her*) death.

Give us understanding that relieves our aching hearts. Help us not to rush through this valley but to walk with you and learn what it means to live and die in your sight. Teach us to trust in your grace in life and in death. Be especially with members of (*name's*) family. Clothe each with comfort, compassion, and love. May they sense your presence through our words and acts no matter how inadequate those may be. And now we trust the spirit of our loved one with you, O God, believing in your promise of eternal life. **Amen.**

(*For healing*)

O God, you have come in Jesus Christ,
    tending to all who are bent in pain,
    to those separated from others by disease
    or bound by death's power.
Come to us now, as tender touch,
    healing balm, and liberating relief.
Urge us to move in new ways;
    encourage us to embrace the discomforts of becoming
    whole; remove from us the fear of relentless pain.
As Jesus spoke to so many and touched your hurting people,
    come now, speak to us, and touch us.
Restore us by your living and amazing grace. **Amen.**

(*During winter*)

Breathe, O God, the fire of your Spirit
    to warm our lives in this season.
We are tired of thermostats and electric blankets,
    layered clothing and dirty snow piles.
Make us aware that even in the dead of winter
    the fire of love can burn within us
    and your grace will bring us once again to springtime.
Amen.

WORSHIP&
DAILY
LIFE

(For daily life)

From birth, O God, you have made us part of other people's lives. These relationships can be confusing, challenging, and rewarding, sometimes all at the same time. Teach us your intention for our relationships. Help us have an open heart to others. **Amen.**

(For daily life)
God,
Give us minds for learning,
   hearts for caring,
      and a desire for both.
Amen.

(For daily life)
Eternal God, who has created all things
   good and beautiful and true,
   teach us so to honor your creative work
   in all we think and say and do,
   that our worship may become seamless with our lives,
   and our lives with your good purposes.
Through Jesus Christ we pray. **Amen.**

(For daily life)
Empty us now of all self-consciousness;
   empty us now of all preoccupation;
   take from us now all of our deepest concerns;
   take from us now all of our words and movement.
Make us yours, yours alone, that you may move us in faith.
   Amen.

(For those who guide children)

What would you have us teach our children? What would you have our children teach us? They are such precious gifts from you and so open to life. Guide us in how to nourish their whole beings. May they learn that our strength comes from you. May we walk with them through joys and difficulties, sharing our awareness of your grace. **Amen.**

(*For daily life*)
God you have formed us and you know us.
Help us trust that you have endowed us with gifts for ministry.
Provide us courage to learn about ourselves
    what you already know.
Light our path, one step at a time.
Reveal each day your divine desire for our lives.
Lead us to see in your creation the needs you can meet
    only through our willingness to hear and obey.
Grant that we may know your redeeming grace in each "failure."
Show us your direction in every apparent dead end; assure us of
    your companionship as we respond to your summons,
    that as we grow to recognize and listen to your loving voice,
    we may come to walk and serve in faith.
By the grace of Jesus Christ. **Amen.**

(*For work*)
Gracious God, as we start this workday we are reminded of the fullness of the day that stretches before us. We are aware of the gift of time and the many things that we will do with this time today. We are aware of the many people our work affects and the web of relationships that encompasses our daily work. We are aware of the needs that our work revolves around. We pray to be attentive to such needs and concerns. **Amen.**

(*For work*)
We ask today that you be with us in the midst of our busy schedule. We know there will be times during this workday when our minds focus away from you and onto the work at hand, but we pray that every action and decision we make is a reflection of our faith in you. Thank you for this day. Thank you for the work at hand. In Christ's name we pray. **Amen.**

WORSHIP&
DAILY
LIFE

(*For work*)

God, we all have work to do.

The infant has to grasp and come to speech and mobility.

The toddler has to enter a battle of wills,
   the discovery of authority, of yes and of no.

The child must play, must enter the human story until
   reenactment becomes reality and costumes become clothes.

The adolescent must discover all the power and tension
   within his or her skin, to be and to connect, to attract and
   repel, to love and serve others.

God, we all have work to do.

Some of us must trade our exertion for currency.

Some of us will be able to market our gifts and skills.

Some of us will by windfall be able to work for fun.

But we all have work to do:
   To love and be loved
   To love and be unnoticed
   To love and be denied
   To share and to receive
   To share and be depleted
   To share and be used
   To forgive and be forgiven
   To forgive and be played the fool
   To forgive and be freed to love
      and share without attachment to results.

God, our work is more like your work than we first imagined
   when we first saw your own Son, Jesus,
   coming as an infant, toddler, child, adolescent, one of us,
   loving, sharing, forgiving—all divine and, yes, human
   work.

God, we all have work to do today, this week, this year.

Move within us, love us, share with us, forgive us, until all
   our work is yours.

Love through us, share through us, forgive through us,

Until all our work is prayer. **Amen.**

(*For daily life*)
Lord, remind us
    that you measure our days
    not in the acquisition of status or wealth,
    not in success or skill,
    but in trusting you.

Help us to see
    all whom we encounter
    as a part of your plan.

Help us to see the stranger on the street
    or the familiar faces at work
    as lives to which you have connected us.

Help us to know that faithfulness
    is seldom more prayer,
    more solitude,
    more work within the walls of the church.

Help us to know that faithfulness
    is giving you access to all that we are,
    all that we do,
    so that together
    we can do your work.

Help us to believe
    that as we give you access to our lives,
    every task we do,
    every person we meet,
    every place we go
    is your work.

Remind us
    that the smallest thing we do
    may be the most important to you.

Help us to see,
    as you see,
    that all of our life
    is the Lord's work.

Amen.

WORSHIP&
DAILY
LIFE

(For parents, grandparents, teachers, and other friends of children)
I stand before you, O God, with so much on my mind.
My responsibilities are great, the tasks before me tremendous,
and I am only me.

So I ask you, O God:
Where can I go when a storm's brewing up?
When others come running to me, and holding them tight I
say, "It's okay," but I worry inside?
Where can I go?

What can I say when a baby bird dies?
When a child looks sorrowfully up and wants to know why?
What can I say?

How can I know when I give others advice
    that the times I say yes and the times I say no
    will lead someone I love to grow healthy and wise?
How can I know?

My responsibilities are great, the tasks before me tremendous,
    and I am only me.

So, I ask you, O God:
Where can I go when a storm's brewing up?
What can I say when a baby bird dies?
How can I know when I give others advice?

(A time for silent reflection followed by these words of assurance)

Leader: You ask, "Where can I go when a storm's brewing up?"

**People: Jesus said, " 'Peace! Be still!' Then the wind ceased, and
there was a dead calm. He said to them, 'Why are you
afraid?' " (Mark 4:39-40)**

Leader: You ask, "What can I say when a baby bird dies?"

**People: Jesus said, "Are not five sparrows sold for two pennies? Yet
not one of them is forgotten in God's sight. But even the
hairs of your head are all counted. Do not be afraid; you
are of more value than many sparrows." (Luke 12:6-7)**

Leader: You ask, "How can I know when I give others advice?"

**People: Jesus said, "All authority in heaven and on earth has
been given to me. Go therefore and make disciples of
all nations, baptizing them in the name of the Father
and of the Son and of the Holy Spirit, and teaching
them to obey everything that I have commanded you.
And remember, I am with you always, to the end of the
age." (Matthew 28:18-20)**

Leader: Trust God in Jesus Christ, who is with you always,
        and do not be afraid.

(For those needing justice and reconciliation)
Into the light of your healing love, O God,
   we lift to you with our hearts
   the injured and wounded of our world
   who have lived in harm's way,
   in the shadow of war,
   in the neighborhood of street violence,
   in the family of shouts and fists,
   in community that cherishes weapons;
   the hungry, who hope for a real meal,
   clean water, and the bread of friendship;
   the humiliated, who have received the scorn of others;
   the tender ones in fragile steps of recovering;
   the sorrowful, who are grieving loss from death and dislocation.

Into the light of your justice and righteousness, O God,
   we lift to you with our hearts
   the wealthy, who forget we are blessed to bless one another;
   the arrogant, who do not see the needs
   of those they pass on their journey;
   the proud, who believe they have done something
   to deserve your bountiful grace;
   the grasping hearts and hands
   that desire more rather than enough.

Into the light of your reconciling grace, O God,
   we lift to you with our hearts
   the ones who by accident of language, culture,
   religion, and land are marginalized;
   the ones who believe we are enemies
   or competitors of one another;
   the ones who believe we are less than
   or more than others in your divine love;
   the ones separated by highways, boundaries,
   neighborhoods, oceans,
   who in our isolation forget
   that you bear unconditional love for us all.

In the light of your grace,
   search us with your divine concern.
   Heal and transform,
   redirect and reconnect all that
   which is broken or crooked within and among us,
   by the presence of your living spirit,
   in Jesus Christ. **Amen.**

Petitions

(An echo song)

Leader: People:

1. God, you are kind and lov - ing, kind and lov - ing let us be.
2. God, you are wise and know -ing, wise and know - ing let us be.
3. God, you are strong but gen - tle, strong but gen - tle let us be.
4. God, you see all things clear - ly, all things clear - ly let us see.
5. God, you are al - ways near me, al - ways near you let me be.

Intercessions

While these prayers of intercession can be used specifically for those named in the italic headings, they can also be used regularly in corporate worship. Consider recognizing a particular area of work and ministry each week, placing symbols of the professions involved on the altar. These prayers can also be used in small-group ministries and other intercessory prayer ministries.

(For those in health and healing professions)

Today we ask for your strength and guidance for those among us who are part of the healing ministries in this community. We know that you have called them to use their gifts to show your love and concern to patients in offices, clinics, emergency rooms, hospitals, and homes.

Their tasks of listening and caring require great patience. Center them, O God. Their work calls for vast attention to detail and immense skill. Guide them to focus their education and abilities to be agents of healing. The hours they work are long and full of stress. O God, we ask that you refresh and strengthen them as they labor.

We thank you that they are in ministry in your name. May they know that no matter how difficult the day, you are also at the patient's side with them. May they know that our community of faith will hold them in prayer. **Amen.**

WORSHIP&
DAILY
LIFE

(For those in law enforcement and social services)

God of justice and mercy, only you know all the hurts and injustices in our community. We praise you that there are those among us who have been called to help the community in its efforts to treat people in a just way. We ask that you be with police, caseworkers, advocates, lawyers, judges, parole officers, prison officials, and others who work with those who have caused harm or are the recipients of harm.

Danger is often present in the lives of those working in law enforcement and social services. May they know security in you. Their decisions are often difficult and the resources too limited. Sustain them in all circumstances. Only you can know what is best for those whom they serve. May they receive wisdom and compassion from you as they work. O God, we thank you for those called to this work, and we ask that they may know your presence and be aware of the prayers offered for them by this community of faith. **Amen.**

(For those who produce food)

O loving God, who transforms the seed into fruit, we pray for those who participate in this mystery of seedtime and harvest. By their hands we receive your daily gifts of sustenance and feast on all your bounty. Help the farmers and the gardeners to prepare the soil, till the ground, plant the seed, and harvest in your name. May they be good caretakers of the earth for others who will follow. When harvests do not come, provide the security and strength needed.

Be with those who tend flocks and herds for provision of food. We pray for all those who take the harvest, market it, and serve us as we obtain the nutrition necessary for health. May they understand their important ministry in supporting life, and may they know that they are ministering to the world with you, O God. We thank you for their call to this work, and we ask that they may know your presence and be aware of the prayers given for them by this community of faith. **Amen.**

(For those who give time without financial compensation)

God of compassion, this day we especially give thanks for those who serve others without receiving payment for their work: those who volunteer to help the homeless, sick, lonely, hungry, disabled, imprisoned, and deprived people of our world; those who work with children and adults to give them new opportunities for learning and development; those who help us be better citizens and keep the important issues before our communities; those who work to save our environment and precious resources; those who spend their time supporting your work in the world with prayer.

Help these givers of gifts rely on you for energy, renewal, and strength. May they be able to walk with those they serve as humble servants in Christ's name. We thank you for their call to this work, and we ask that they may know your presence and be aware of the prayers given for them by this community of faith. **Amen.**

(For those in banking, business, and service industries)

God, we thank you that there are those you have called to serve through commerce. Through the intricate matters that they must handle, help them to remain faithful to your love. May they see each customer as one of your children.

Help them to ask the difficult questions that need to be asked. Help them to be dissatisfied with quick gain over long-needed results. Guide them to use resources wisely. Strengthen their resolve to use their gifts in service to you and others. May they help their coworkers find joy in service. We thank you for their call to this work, and we ask that they be aware of your presence and be strengthened by the prayers given for them by this community of faith. **Amen.**

(For friends who lose their jobs)

God, we are aware that friends in this community have lost their jobs. The gifts you have given them are no longer needed in their place of work. We come to you with the pain they are feeling and the pain we are feeling with them. While some of us are trying to decide when to retire, they have been forced to retire—for a time, at least. Sustain them in the knowledge that they did their jobs well and that their work was pleasing to you. We pray that they and their families may feel the assurance of your love for them. In Jesus' name we pray. **Amen.**

WORSHIP&
DAILY
L I F E

(For the employed and the unemployed)

O Lord, our mighty rock and provider, we come at this time to pray for those who are without employment, those who are new arrivals to the work force, those who are changing careers, and those who are anxious to advance in their chosen fields.

Lord, for those in search of employment, let them discover what jobs are available. Match perfectly employer and employee. For those who are just arriving in the work force, help them to carry out the duties and responsibilities of the jobs that have been assigned to them.

For those seeking to change careers, help them get the education and acquire the skills needed to qualify for the job desired. And for those who desire to advance, give them the willingness to be open to change, and the understanding that new jobs bring new duties. In all cases, Lord, let these people's desires be tailored to coincide with your divine purpose for their lives. In Christ's name we pray. **Amen.**

(For those who work and for those who hire)

Lord, who is an ever-present help in time of trouble, we pray on behalf of all those who work and who hire in our society, asking that you let justice roll down like a mighty stream in the workplace. Let those who are working give an honest day's work and those who are hiring give wages that are fair. And, Lord, if there is injustice anywhere, lend your powerful hand to bring equity into being. We have seen your mighty hand at work and know that you are the same God yesterday, today, and tomorrow. In you, O God, do we continue to put our trust, and in Jesus' name we pray. **Amen.**

(For those who serve others)

Lord, you are one who heals, who shields, who forms the hearts and minds of all; open our eyes to see one another, our ears to hear one another's cries. Let us not think of ourselves more highly than we ought. Help us to appreciate the work that others do. Let us open our hearts to the garbage collector, those who wash cars by hand, the pharmacist who prepares our medicine, and those who repair bad mufflers.

God, strengthen the hands and feet of barbers and hairdressers. Lord, let us who sleep in hotels be more courteous to the housekeepers and the waiters. Help us to recognize the dignity in all work. In Christ's name we pray. **Amen.**

(*For everyone who works*)
Leader: We pray this day for all who labor,

People: which includes all of us.

Leader: For those who work with their hands.

People: For those who work with their minds.

Leader: For those who work with their families.

People: For those who look for work.

Leader: For those who seek to find their next meal.

People: For those who help others find their next meal.

Leader: For those who care for their homes.

People: For those who give away their time freely.

Leader: For those who work to live.

People: For those who live to work.

Leader: All of us are given work.

People: Let us thank the Lord no matter what the work.

All: Amen.

(*For those who teach*)
Right: We pray for teachers who
wipe tears and give hugs,
welcome laughter and smile often,
touch hearts and open minds.

Left: We pray for teachers who
equip us for the possibilites of the future,
challenge us to consider new ideas,
encourage us to do our best.

Right: We pray for teachers who
prepare carefully despite crowded schedules,
create amazing things from limited resources,
work long hours and receive little recognition.

Left: We pray for teachers who are
called to a holy task,
created in the image of God,
empowered to transform lives.

All: In the name of Jesus the Great Teacher,
we pray for teachers. Amen.

WORSHIP &

(For those being baptized)

A child, pure as gold, gift from God, miracle of life, is claimed this day as yours, Parent God. May *(name)* know your abundant love along every step of life. Strengthen and guide these parents, who devote their lives to *(name's)* care. Give us all the skills and commitment we need to teach *(name)* your ways, and the desire to model our reliance on you every day of our lives. May *(name)* experience your love through those who love and care for *her/him.* In the name of Jesus we pray. **Amen.**

(Following the baptismal formula at the time of the laying on of hands)
(Name), may the hands of God hold you.
May God bless the hands that touch and care for you.
May God guide the hands that will teach you.
May God lead the hands that will send you forth in ministry.
May God strengthen the hands that will, in love
    and in season, let you go as you grow,
that born of the spirit, you may die and rise with Christ in
    the power of God's Spirit. **Amen.**

(For the natural world)
Creator God, we pray
    for the oceans and all the creatures that live there;
    for the continents that rise above the waters;
    for the holy continuity of creation,
    in which mountains erupt and erode,
    plant communities encroach and subside,
    species arrive and depart;
    for the living stage of this fragile earth,
    upon which we build and travel, arrive and depart.
We pray your guidance for all we use and serve.
Move us to respect all weather;
    remind us to cherish all seasons;
Push us to conserve water and air,
    atmosphere and tributaries.
Shape our care for all you create;
    help us come to respect all that we do not yet understand.
Bless all who will follow us here. **Amen.**

Great Thanksgivings

As a part of the service of Holy Communion, the Great Thanksgiving is our proclamation of God's action throughout history. These prayers of the priestly people embrace the action of God in the goodness of daily life, while keeping the basic structure of ecumenical eucharistic prayer.

The Lord be with you.
And also with you.
Lift up your hearts.
We lift them up to the Lord.
Let us give thanks to the Lord our God.
It is right to give our thanks and praise.

It is right, and a good and joyful thing,
    always and everywhere to give thanks to you,
    Father Almighty, creator of heaven and earth.

We thank you, God, for the wonderful work of creation, for electrons and elephants, for bayous and butterflies, for the colors of the rainbow and the colors of our skin, for the stars and starfish.

You formed us in your image
    and breathed into us the breath of life.

We praise you that your work is our life. We live because you made us. We live as your artwork. We live as your masterpiece. We live as your treasure and your handiwork.

When we turned away, and our love failed,
    your love remained steadfast.
You delivered us from captivity,
    made covenant to be our sovereign God,
    and spoke to us through the prophets.

WORSHIP&
DAILY
LIFE

And so,
  with your people on earth
  and all the company of heaven
  we praise your name and join their unending hymn:

Holy, holy, holy Lord, God of power and might,
heaven and earth are full of your glory.
  Hosanna in the highest.
Blessed are those who work in the name of the Lord.
Hosanna in the highest.

Thank you for your Son, Jesus Christ, who by his life
  redeemed our daily life and by his work made all our work
  blessed. His birth was witnessed by shepherds who took
  time off work to attend his birth. He worked as a carpenter. He invited ordinary fishermen to become extraordinary
  fishers for and with God. He told stories of farm workers
  and homemakers, invited tax collectors to become disciples, and saw worth in work that others despised. He
  cooked the disciples Easter breakfast.

By his work he taught us to see your glory in ordinary events.
By his ministry he showed us that compassion is our life work.
By his vocation he followed God's will and invited us to follow him.
By his death and resurrection he redeemed us and revealed
  that our work is never lost, never without purpose, never
  worthless.

On the night in which he gave himself up for us,
  he took bread, gave thanks to you, broke the bread,
  gave it to his disciples, and said:
"Take, eat; this is my body which is given for you.
Do this in remembrance of me."

When the supper was over, he took the cup,
  gave thanks to you, gave it to his disciples, and said:
"Drink from this, all of you;
  this is my blood of the new covenant,
  poured out for you and for many for the forgiveness of sins.
Do this, as often as you drink it,
  in remembrance of me."

And so,
in remembrance of these your mighty acts in Jesus Christ,
we offer ourselves as workers in your mission,
  and promise in our workplace and daily life
  to witness to the truth that

Christ has died; Christ is risen; Christ will come again.

(*Continue with "Service of Word and Table 1." See pages 36–39* of The United Methodist Book of Worship.)

The Lord be with you.
And also with you.
Lift up your hearts. (*The pastor may lift hands and keep them raised.*)
We lift them up to the Lord.
Let us give thanks to the Lord our God.
It is right to give our thanks and praise.

It is right, and a good and joyful thing,
   always and everywhere to give thanks to you,
   Almighty God, creator of heaven and earth.
You formed us in your image
   and breathed into us the breath of life.
You placed us in the earth-garden and charged us
   to care for it as the object of your love and delight.
When we took from the earth
   for our own advantage,
   you sent us away to toil and to search for you.
Yet your love remained steadfast.
When you saw our bitter yoke and oppression,
   you heard our cry, delivered us from captivity,
   made covenant to be our sovereign God.
You spoke to us through the prophets,
   who yearned for a day of vocation
   when you would give us to be a light to the nations,
   that your salvation would reach to the ends of the earth.

And so,
with your people on earth
   and all the company of heaven
   we praise your name and join their unending hymn:

Holy, holy, holy Lord, God of power and might,
heaven and earth are full of your glory.
   Hosanna in the highest.
Blessed is he who comes in the name of the Lord.
   Hosanna in the highest.

(*Continue with "Service of Word and Table 1." See pages 36–39* of The United Methodist Book of Worship.)

WORSHIP&
DAILY
LIFE

The Lord be with you.
And also with you.
Lift up your hearts. (*The pastor may lift hands and keep them raised.*)
We lift them up to the Lord.
Let us give thanks to the Lord our God.
It is right to give our thanks and praise.

It is right, and a good and joyful thing,
    always and everywhere to give thanks to you,
    Almighty God, creator of heaven and earth.

We praise you for all who labor for the common good
    and for those whose service is unappreciated.
 We thank you for children whose play is the work of learning
    to live in the world.
We thank you for disciples who are obedient
    to the promptings of your Spirit in all their relationships.
We thank you for your yearning mercy
    that waits for us to make all our hours and days participation
    in your healing and blessing of the earth and all peoples.

You made us in your image
    and set us in a lush garden as caretakers.
When we chose to have it all to ourselves,
    you turned our freedom to the toil for survival.
When we cried out in our misery,
    you delivered us from captivity
    and made covenant to be our sovereign God.
By the prophets you called us to return to you
    and delight in good food without price.
You confronted us with the waste of laboring without you,
    and you asked us,
"Why do you spend your money for that which is not bread,
    and your labor for that which does not satisfy? . . .
Incline your ear, and come to me;
    listen, so that you may live" (Isaiah 55:2-3).

And so,
    with your people on earth
    and all the company of heaven,
    we praise your name and join their unending hymn:

Holy, holy, holy Lord, God of power and might,
heaven and earth are full of your glory.
    Hosanna in the highest.
Blessed is he who comes in the name of the Lord.
    Hosanna in the highest.

Holy are you, and blessed is your Son Jesus Christ.
Anointed with your Spirit,
   his food was to do your will and to complete it.
He took the common things of daily life,
   blessed them, and broke and shared them
   so that all were satisfied.
He told those who followed him,
   "Do not work for the food that perishes,
   but for the food that endures for eternal life."
He confronted the powers of greed and evil
   at the cost of his life,
   but you triumphed over death
   and placed him at your right hand
   to intercede for his disciples until the feast of eternal life.
By water and the Spirit he calls us to continue his work
   until we and all peoples feast at his heavenly banquet.

On the night in which he gave himself up for us,
   he took bread, gave thanks to you, broke the bread,
   gave it to his disciples, and said:
"Take, eat; this is my body which is given for you.
Do this in remembrance of me."

When the supper was over, he took the cup,
   gave thanks to you, gave it to his disciples, and said:
"Drink from this, all of you;
   this is my blood of the new covenant,
   poured out for you and for many for the forgiveness of sins.
Do this, as often as you drink it,
   in remembrance of me."

And so,
in remembrance of these your mighty acts in Jesus Christ,
we offer ourselves to live daily
   as a holy and living sacrifice,
   in union with Christ's offering for us,
as we proclaim the mystery of faith.

Christ has died; Christ is risen; Christ will come again.

(*Continue with "Service of Word and Table 1." See pages 36–39
of* The United Methodist Book of Worship.)

WORSHIP&
DAILY
LIFE

The Lord be with you.
And also with you.
Lift up your hearts.
We lift them up to the Lord.
Let us give thanks to the Lord our God.
It is right to give our thanks and praise.

It is a good and fruitful work to give thanks to you,
Almighty God, in all places and at all times
and in all our tasks.
In our cars, our homes, our offices, our fields, and our
kitchens;
at our tables, our desks, our telephones, and computers;
when we are resting or waiting, laboring or supervising,
following or leading.
All these we do with all your people now on earth and all the
multitude of heaven, praising your name
and joining in their unending hymn:

Holy, holy, holy Lord, God of power and might,
heaven and earth are full of your glory.
Hosanna in the highest.
Blessed is he who comes in the name of the Lord.
Hosanna in the highest.

Holy are you and holy is your work among us in Jesus Christ,
who came to be born in the home of a carpenter,
a trade he learned and practiced,
a laborer in our midst.
He called out fishermen and activists.
He healed the servant of a soldier.
He received the support of resourceful women.
He delegated his ministry to his disciples,
empowered all his followers
to do his divine work in this world.
By his suffering, death, and resurrection,
you gave birth to your church,
delivered us from the bondage of sin
and the power of death,
and made with us a new covenant by water and the Spirit.

On the night in which he gave himself up for us,
he took bread, gave thanks to you, broke the bread,
gave it to his disciples, and said:
"Take, eat; this is my body which is given for you.
Do this in remembrance of me."

When the supper was over, he took the cup,
  gave thanks to you, gave it to his disciples, and said:
"Drink from this, all of you;
  this is my blood of the new covenant,
  poured out for you and for many for the forgiveness of sins.
Do this, as often as you drink it,
  in remembrance of me."

And so as a baptized and commissioned people,
  remembering your mighty work in Jesus Christ,
we offer ourselves, our daily lives,
  and our unique locations
  for ministry in the world—
  homes and hospitals, parks and stores,
  prisons and concert halls—
  as a living and holy sacrifice
  in union with Christ's offering for us
as we proclaim the mystery of faith.

Christ has died; Christ is risen; Christ will come again.

*(Continue with "Service of Word and Table 1." See pages 36–39
of* The United Methodist Book of Worship.)

Dedications

Dedicating gifts is more than praying over money. These prayers of dedication recognize that all of life is a gift from God and that we are called to use that gift in ways that honor our Creator.

These gifts that we bring, O God,
   are a response to your love.
Your provision for us is constant;
   your faithfulness is never-ending;
   your love continually breaks through to us.
May our giving be worthy in your sight.
May our whole lives be a response to you. **Amen.**

O God, teach us how to give.
We sense that deep within us there is a desire to share,
But so often we hold back in hesitancy and fear.
May we truly learn to rely on you, believing that in giving
   we will receive all that is needed for our lives,
   that through our giving others will receive
   what is needed for their lives. **Amen.**

Holy God, just as wheat scattered over the fields
   is gathered in to make our daily bread,
   so we bring these fruits of our labors
   that we might share in the work of your new creation.
Amen.

**WORSHIP&
DAILY
LIFE**

We have placed, O Lord, our offerings before you.
You know their source, the labor they represent.
May we in this community of faith
  learn to be generous people.
For you, O Giver of Life, have taught us
  through your Son, Jesus Christ,
  that when we give our lives away, we shall find them.
Help us to find life in you. **Amen.**

O Giver of Time, renewed each day with the rising of the sun,
We ask for wisdom in how we use the minutes
  and hours granted to us.
May we be generous in using time for acts of
  compassion and mercy.
May we find a rhythm of work, rest, leisure,
  and Sabbath that reflects your will for our lives.
Daily may our lives reflect to others your peace and joy.
O Giver of Time, we dedicate our time to your service. **Amen.**

God of money and minds, savings and service, land and
love. We come at this time to honor you with our substance. As we leave may we glorify you through our service.
All we have, Lord, we give to you. Accept these offerings.
May we always remember the source from which they have
come. **Amen.**

When you baptized us into the death and resurrection of
your Son, O God, you claimed all of us—our hearts, our
minds, our work, and our leisure. Help us not to play it safe
by giving only money. With these gifts we give ourselves
anew. Use the gifts. Use the givers. We are yours, through
Christ our Lord. **Amen.**

In your holy presence, we offer our presence.
Through your loving service, we offer our service.
Receiving your bountiful gifts, we offer our gifts.
Because of your life poured out for us in Christ,
  we offer ourselves and all our lives as prayer. **Amen.**

Sending Forth

The act of sending forth is not a liturgical device to bring closure to a worship service. Rather it extends worship, moving the gathered community out into the world in active praise and thanksgiving. As we are sent forth, we are challenged to make all of our life worship. It is appropriate for a deacon, if present, or an assisting minister to send the congregation forth to love and serve the Lord in daily life.

Rise, shine, for your light has come
  and the Spirit of the Lord has risen upon you.
You are blessed.
Now go and be a blessing!

Leader: Sisters and brothers, whom will you see this week?
      What will they need? Will you dare to see their
      need and love them with the love of Christ? In
      Christ's name go and be good news!
People: We are sent in Christ's name! Thanks be to God!

You have come;
You have heard;
You have listened.
May your understanding cause you to respond.
Go forth into the world and dare to make a difference.

WORSHIP&
DAILY
LIFE

Leader: What does the Lord require of you as you go from this place but to do justice, to love mercy, and to walk peacefully with God? In the name of Jesus Christ, go to serve God and your neighbor in all that you do.

People: Thanks be to God!

Sisters and brothers, God does not ask you to
    go to far off places.
God sends you back to people and places you do know.
God sends you in the power of the Spirit.
Go where the kind word is needed.
Go where the risk of love will make a difference.
Put your feet in the street and go!

Note: Particularly appropriate during the Great Fifty Days of Easter

Children of God, you are not alone as you go.
Like a pillar of fire and a cloud of glory, the Lord goes
    before you.
Where there is hurt and need, stop to see the hand of God.
Do not be afraid. Take heart.
I send you in the name of Jesus, our Passover.

Leader: The Good Shepherd asks, "Do you love me?"
People: "Yes, Lord, you know we love you."
Leader: "Then tend my lambs," the Shepherd says.
        Go out in tender mercy. The liturgy continues!
People: Thanks be to God! Alleluia!

Sisters and brothers, we are not dismissed.
We are not just free to go.
Christ sends us!
Go in the power of the Spirit
    to love and serve the Lord.
Go to help and heal in all you do.
Thanks be to God!

Go home. Make welcome the stranger in your midst!
Go work. Create spaces of justice and mercy!
Go learn. Sharpen the talents God has given you!
Go play. Rejoice in the wonder of God's creation!

Leader: Lord, your love has brought us here,
People: By your love send us forth.
Leader: May your love be active in us
as we wake or sleep, work or rest, serve or wait.
People: Draw us by the needs of others into the way, the truth, and the life we see in Christ.
All: We follow in faith. Amen.

Go now in peace, for God sends you forth to serve in your community, walks with you on the journey, and meets you when you get there. Go now in peace. **Amen.**

Leader: As we go forth from this place of worship
People: Out into the world of work and life,
Leader: Let us carry with us God's armor of faith
People: To protect us from the evils of our world,
Leader: To move us to have compassion in the world,
People: To provide spiritual strength for the journey.
Leader: The blessings of our Lord go with you always.
People: And also with you.
All: Amen.

Leader: As we have been touched by the hand of God today,
People: Let us take this touch into all that we do this week.
Leader: In our homes and families, may that touch mean togetherness and care.
People: In our places of work, may that touch mean honesty and integrity.
Leader: In our communities, may that touch mean commitment and justice.
People: We are the people of God.
Leader: And we are called to make a difference in our world. Go now in the peace of Jesus Christ.
All: Amen.

WORSHIP& DAILY LIFE

Leader: Worship has drawn you inward to the depths of your own spirit.

People: Our Lord now draws us outward, to a world that needs God's life-giving message.

Leader: You have been transformed by the power of the risen Lord.

People: We go into the world to spread the transforming love of God.

All: **Amen.**

Leader: The font that has called us near
now sends us to our calling.

People: God's blessing on the work.

Leader: The table that has served us well
now leads us to our serving.

People: God's blessing on the work.

Leader: The Word that has given us life
now guides us to our living.

People: God's blessing on the work.

By faith we say that we do not leave this place alone.
And by faith we say that our ministries are led by Another.
It is God who goes before us in the life of self-giving.
God it is who leads us on the way
   and makes of us companions in the work.
"Vaya con Dios," we say, then, "Go with God."
Where God goes, we go too.
And where we go, we invite God there.
Go with God
Vaya con Dios. **Amen.**

For all we lift our hands to do,
For all we raise our voices to say,
For all we see on our journey,
Lord, use us.

Particular Days & Occasions

Sometimes in the faith community we act as if secular and civic holidays and celebrations do not exist. Because they are not explicitly Christian in their origin, we ignore them in our worship life. And sometimes in the faith community we seem to order our worship lives around these secular celebrations rather than around the life, death, and resurrection of our Lord. The prayers and other acts of worship in this chapter recognize that civic holidays and secular events are a part of our lives but that God is at the center of our lives.

(*For near Halloween*)
What are the monsters that you fear in your life?
   (*name silently*)
What masks do you wear in order to hide your true self?
   (*name silently*)
Help us, O God,
   not to be afraid of life's darkness.
May we walk through our nights
   with confidence that the monsters before us
   will wither by the power of your love.
Strengthen us to shed our masks
   that the world might know the people
you have created us to be. **Amen.**

WORSHIP&
DAILY
LIFE

(An affirmation of birthday celebrations)

Right: We celebrate God's gift of birth!

Left: We celebrate with those who blow out one candle then dive into the cake with fingers, face, and tongue all at once. They know how to experience life.

Right: We celebrate with those who are turning five and six years old and are filled with excitement about starting school, riding a two-wheeler, and tying shoes without help. They teach us the joy of learning.

Left: We celebrate with those who prefer a party with friends rather than with parents as they try to figure out how they ought to dress, what music to listen to, and who they were born to be. They show us how to seek truth and understanding.

Right: We celebrate with those whose birthday marks the beginning of adulthood, with privileges and responsibilities they have never had before. They remind us of the freedom and the fear that is part of every new opportunity.

Left: We celebrate with those who cannot figure out where the years have gone. The children have grown, but they haven't felt themselves getting any older. They know the challenges of living life to its fullest.

Right: We celebrate with those who no longer count candles but rather the people they love. They know the greatest blessings of life.

All: Every age is a gift from God. We rejoice for all of God's mercies as they unfold throughout the years.

(For Valentine's Day)

May we come to understand, O God, that you are more in love with us than we have ever been with another human being. While we try to balance our time between loved ones and other demands, you are with us always. While we make up with another after an argument, you give total forgiveness. While we sometimes shrink in embarrassment over something someone says, you die because of us and rise again in spite of us. Purify our love to more closely resemble your divine love for us. **Amen.**

(For Mother's Day or Father's Day)
God, our Creator,
We give you thanks for those who have been
   (mothers/fathers) for us.
Help us inherit from them
   that which will make us more fully your people.
Where they have offered us blessings of love,
   may we incorporate those gifts into our lives.
Where they have hurt us or fallen short of our expectations,
   may we learn from them,
   that we might not repeat their mistakes.
May the honor we convey toward our *(mothers/fathers)*
   reflect the honor that we feel toward you.
Amen.

(For Independence Day)
Like fireworks against a night sky,
may your love for us, O God,
explode within us,
that our lives would burst forth
with the flame of your Holy Spirit
and shower the earth
with celebrations of the freedom
we find in Jesus Christ.
Amen.

(For Thanksgiving Day)
God of plenty in the wilderness,
   we bless you for the feast you spread in our daily lives.
On a day of feasting,
   we remember our complaints through the year.
When we thought what we were doing was unimportant,
   you were making good meals,
   touching hurting hearts and bodies,
   opening doors for curious minds,
   telling truth in ways that invited fresh awareness,
   and preparing the way for changed attitudes.
You have spread a table in the wilderness!
Thank you, God.

WORSHIP&
DAILY
LIFE

(For the start of a school year)
New crayons,
   God is with us.
Getting up early,
   God is with us.
Remembering which bus to take,
   God is with us.
Names to learn,
   God is with us.
Homework,
   God is with us.
In all we do
   God is with us.

(For those who save their work)
   You, God, save us. Just as we save files on the computer to prevent them from being lost, so your grace saves us so that we will not be lost. Just as we save files so that we may finish working on them, so you are always busy working on us. Remind us that we are not saved onto disks that will fail or be erased or deleted or destroyed. We are saved in the heart and mind of God. You, O God, do not delete us. You do not lose us. You do not misplace us. Sometimes, God, we forget that we are saved. But like our computers, which save our files even when we are not working, so your grace is always saving us—even when we are not aware of your presence. **Amen.**

(For entering silence)
   Into your divine hands we offer our imaginations and feelings, our thoughts and concerns, our busy distractions. Take them now, and keep them for us so that we might now come to rest in your presence. Draw from us only that which you, God, need from us at this moment. **Amen.**

(*A haiku for the earth*)
The earth groans in pain.
Good stewards we have not been.
"Save me!" cries the earth.

(*Celebrating a new family member*)
What a blessing from you, O God. A new life among us! We celebrate your gift of love, this child, and ask that your tender care surround *him/her*.

Give us the wisdom to know that you have given us an opportunity to learn to love again. May we love as you would have us love.

Give us the hearts to know that you have given us the opportunity to learn compassion again. May we show compassion as you are compassionate to us.

Help us to live in ways that this child will come to know and love you all the days of *his/her* life. We celebrate this new life with grateful hearts. **Amen.**

(*For a political election*)
Wise and wonder-filled God, another election is upon us. It is an opportunity of freedom won with difficulty and hardship, still not available to all.

We infrequently appreciate our voting privileges and reluctantly participate. Forgive us. The lives of your children everywhere are at stake, for we are all affected by decisions made by world and local leaders. Help us lay aside the rhetoric of the campaigns and make our decisions on the basis of what values the candidates represent.

Give us wisdom to sort out what is really meant by the words spoken. Subdue our apathy and cynicism, our reluctance to take a stand. Get us moving, God, out of our living rooms into the risk-filled political world. Help us understand that voting is a way of living out our faith in you and making a difference in this world.

In the name of Jesus we pray. **Amen.**

WORSHIP&
DAILY
LIFE

(A litany for love of the earth)

Leader: God the creator, today we celebrate
all of your marvelous creation.

People: And God saw that it was good.

Leader: The vast universe, the stars and planets,
and the planet we call home, our earth,

People: And God saw that it was good.

Leader: The purity of the air that we breathe,
that sustains all life,

People: And God saw that it was good.

Leader: The seas and bodies of water
that provide a rich bounty,

People: And God saw that it was good.

Leader: The fertile soil that gives forth life,

People: And God saw that it was good.

Leader: The plant life and trees
that contribute to the air we breathe,

People: And God saw that it was good.

Leader: The animals and all living creatures
that walk upon our earth,

People: And God saw that it was good.

Leader: Humanity, whom God called upon
to take responsibility for this earth,

People: We who are entrusted as stewards of all,

Leader: We must care enough to repair and
sustain this gift of our planet earth.

**People: We humans who at our worst
destroy and exploit the planet.**

Leader: We humans who at our best, live in harmony
with all of life and seek to care for all life.

**People: God saw everything that God had made, and indeed,
it was very good.**

All: Amen.

(Litany for saving the earth)

Leader: God created the heavens and the earth
and called them good.

People: Inspire us to care for your creation, O God.

Leader: God created the darkness and the light
and called them good.

People: Inspire us to care for your creation, O God.

Leader: God created the waters and the dry land
and called them good.

People: Inspire us to care for your creation, O God.

Leader: God created the fish of the sea, the birds of the air,
and the creatures of the dry land.

People: Inspire us to care for your creation, O God.

Leader: God created the sun for the morning
and the moon at night.

People: Inspire us to care for your creation, O God.

Leader: God created humankind in God's own likeness.

**People: Inspire us to care for our bodies as temples
of your Holy Spirit, O God.**

Leader: The heavens are filled with smog and the dry land is
strewn with trash and toxic waste.

**People: Inspire us, O God, to be advocates for environmental
protection laws, to buy less, to take public transporta-
tion, and to use products that do not harm the air or
earth.**

Leader: Waterway pollution has killed the fish,
and the birds have trouble finding food.

**People: Inspire us, O God, to feed the birds and small creatures
in our own backyard and to recycle everything we can.**

Leader: Our bodies suffer from eating too much,
exercising too little, and daily stress.

**People: Inspire us, O God, to eat the right amount of nutritious
food and to discover the benefits of moving and using
our bodies as we are able.**

Leader: Today we commit our lives to caring for the earth
and all that is upon it.

People: All creation is yours, O God. Inspire us. Amen.

WORSHIP& DAILY LIFE

(A naming prayer)

Creator, you have made me from the earth. Before I was born, you shaped me. You know when I lie down to sleep and awake in the morning.

You have given me a new name.

You know the work I do with my hands and the roles of my life. You give meaning to even the ordinary things of life.

You have given me a new name.

You know my mind and my thoughts. You know the things I do well and the things I try to hide. You know the person I appear to be and the person I am.

You have given me a new name.

Others told me who I was. I wore my sins and fears like names until I became them.

You have given me a new name.

I have given you my strengths. You have asked that I give you my brokenness so that you might shine through.

You have given me a new name.

Remove those things that separate me from you. Help me not to fear those things that you seem to leave untouched. They keep me holding your hand.

You have given me a new name.

You sustain me with food others may not see. You have erected a monument in my honor. You have placed a new name on the stone. You and I alone know the meaning of the name.

***You* have given me a new name.**
You have given *me* a new name.
You have given me a *new name*.

(Washing and anointing of the hands)
Note: Anointing in biblical times was a public act of selection or setting apart, invoking the Lord's blessing for a specific calling or task. In our times the anointing of the hands serves as an acknowledgment that as Christians, whose lives are open to the leadership of God, all of the tasks of our lives are the Lord's work.

*A decision for Jesus Christ, or a deeper walk of faith, may allow some people to see their work and daily life, for the first time, as part of God's work. The first of these small rituals may be used as a cleansing or renewal ritual (a point of departure from self-centered daily life). The second may be used as a consecration of daily life. These may be used together or individually. An excellent hymn to sing during such rituals is "Bless Thou the Gifts" (*The United Methodist Hymnal, *587).*

Washing of Hands

Each station requires two assistants. One holds a pitcher of water and the other a basin or receptacle. Members of the faith community come and hold their hands over the basin. A small amount of water is poured over their hands. As the water is poured over each person's hands, the person responds by saying:
**We bring these hands to you
for the Lord's work.**

Anointing of hands

Members of the faith community may simply open their hands, palms upward. The worship leader, or those designated, make the sign of the cross on the palm of each hand as they say:
**Spirit of God,
use these hands
as your own**.

(Ritual for the passage to adulthood)
Note: The specific age that one is considered an adult varies from culture to culture. This ritual can be used at whatever age is appropriate for your community. The ritual may include words of challenge and encouragement given by spiritual leaders in the faith community. A symbolic gift to adulthood may also be given, such as a family heirloom, a Bible, or a checking account opened in the person's name.

Leader: *(Name)*, we celebrate your passage to adulthood.

People: It is a time for celebration, and we are grateful to witness this passage.

Parent(s): We have tried to raise you with the values that have been important to us. We realize that we have not always lived up to these values, but our intentions have been sincere. More than anything, we have wanted you to grow straight and true.

Individual: I am more grateful for your loving care than I can express in words. I pray that I will be able to live daily the values that you have taught me.

Parent(s): We have also tried to raise you with a deep and personal Christian faith. We pray that this faith will sustain you and guide you in all you do.

Individual: I am thankful that you have raised me in the Christian faith, for such faith will lead me.

Parent(s): We realize that the world can be a harsh and cruel place, but there will also be much to savor and love on your journey.

Individual: You have taught me the ways of survival, but also the transforming power of love.

Parent(s): We celebrate the person you have become and the journey that lies ahead of you.

Individual: I will go forth, taking with me the gifts of love and faith that you have given me.

Parent(s): Remember that however far you travel from us and your original home, we are always here for you.

Individual: And now I, in my adulthood, am here for you.

Parent(s): We love you.

Individual: I love you.

Prayers for Personal Use

The other sections of this book are intended primarily for use in corporate worship. The prayers in this section are personal prayers for use in daily life.

Good morning, God. Thank you for the sleep. Today is a new day. Even though the list of chores is long and the list of obligations even greater, and though I am no more organized today than last night, today you have given me a fresh start. For the alarm clock's call is loud and shrill and pulls me unwillingly out of a dead sleep. Your call is no less awakening. You, O God, call me to live this day full of wonder and delight, knowing that I have been given another day to live with and for you. Amen.

Dearest Lord, you have seen me through another workday. Thank you for your presence and companionship during the day. Thank you for your help and strength in getting through this day. Thank you for coworkers and people who support my work. Thank you for patience and understanding. Thank you for people who forgive my mistakes, and grant me the ability to forgive others who make mistakes. Amen.

You have spoken my name, O God.
I turn to find your face
and see a world that says, "I am here."

You have spoken my name, O God.
I look to ask, "What task have I to do?"
And you are there in my looking,
speaking purpose in all my tasks.

You have sung my name, O God.
I searched for a place to sing to you.
You made the song swell within me
until I sang where I was.

You have sung my name, O God.
I search for words to sing to you,
and you wash my soul in music
until I sing, forgetting words.

You have written my name, O God.
I looked for where it was written.
You opened your hand
and it was there.

O God who knows my name,
Who gives meaning to all I do,
Who fills me with song wherever I am,
Who writes my name in the sky and the earth,
I give you thanks.

Lord, I praise thee, I honor thee, I magnify your Holy name. Lord, if I had ten thousand tongues, they would not be enough to give you all the honor and glory due thee. Therefore, Lord, as I rise from my slumber and go about the business of this world, I thank you for strength to let my life become prayer. Thank you for eyes that are open to see the needs of the world and ears to hear the cries of the needy. Now, Lord, as I seek to link my faith with the needs of the world, thank you for your ever present love and guidance. In Jesus' name I pray. Amen.

God, I'm late. The alarm didn't go off. My life is a rush. In my haste, be with me. Do not let me hurt someone. Do not let me do something really dumb. Help me not to be thoughtless. Slow me down—just a little. Amen.

O God, I look for you among those who cross my path. I sense that you are walking with me, willing me the joys of the Kingdom. May I see all I meet as family—your family, O God. Help me to be loving parent, sister, brother, grandparent to those seeking the affirmation of relationship. May I accept the love others extend to me. Help me to undergird my life in prayer to serve you in all I think, say, and do. Amen.

Dear God, the morning is cold but the shower is hot. The water feels good. I feel new and clean. O God, make my soul as clean as my body. As I brush off of my teeth the stains of yesterday, may you also brush yesterday's stains from my soul. As I shampoo the roots of my hair, may your grace clean the roots of my soul. As I flush away all of yesterday's poisons, may your redemptive power flush away all the poisons that contaminate my soul. As I beautify my body, may you beautify my soul. As I make over my appearance, may you make over my inner looks. Amen.

Loving God, I give you back this day. I had hoped to live each hour without regret, but as I remember the words said, the opportunities lost, the lack of energy for my work, I come asking that you somehow take it all and repair the harm I may have done. Why is it that I stray from your presence when there is such peace and joy in knowing that you are near? I want to learn to live my life without regrets, O God; but I know it is only through walking with you that that can be possible. Strengthen me with rest this night, and help me accept your guidance in all I do tomorrow. Amen.

Awaken me, precious Lord, from my deep spiritual slumber. Enable my heart to long for you as a ship longs for the sea. Only you know that my spiritual senses have been dulled. My world of facts and figures, of production schedules and deadlines, of pressures and conflicts has robbed me of my vision of you and what life should be like. I am in need of your presence. I am in need of your spirit. I am in need of you! Come to me and let me drink of the living waters that you offer. Let me drink deeply of the living well of your spirit. Let me drink and be satisfied. Amen.

WORSHIP & DAILY LIFE

O God,
when I have to face the bully
and those who make fun of me,
be with me
just as you were with Daniel when he was
thrown into the lion's den.
Help me to become a stronger
and more loving person.
Amen.

God,
my parents do not love each other any more.
They fight a lot,
and they don't want to live in the same house.
Sometimes I feel very alone.
Be with me, God.
Help me to love both Mom and Dad.
Be with them too, God.
Help them to know that you still love them.
Amen.

God,
when I am in school,
   help me to be kind to others.
When I sit at my desk to do my work,
   help me to learn about your world.
When I eat in the lunchroom,
   help me to feel thankful for the food.
When I go out for recess,
   help me to be fair in my play.
When I hand in my papers,
   help me to feel that I have done my best work.
When I don't know the answers,
   help me to be patient.
When the dismissal bell rings,
   help me to know that you have been in school with me.

Dear God, I really want to win this game. Could you help me? I know you love the other team. I know you love me even when I ask for things that I shouldn't. I know you don't choose sides. I know you let us play the game, but could you lead a cheer for me? Could you run with me? Could you play with me? I want to do my best, and I know I'll only really do my best if you are with me. Help me not to hate the other team and not to wish them bad luck. Play with me. Run with me. Help me. Amen.

Lord, it is my neighbor's first job for pay.
She is sixteen.
Today she is a cashier at the grocery store;
    maybe she will be a loan officer in a bank one day.
Or maybe she will work in a human resources office
    matching people's gifts with the world's great need.
All I know is how good it felt to me when she invited my wife
    and me to come through her checkout line.
She looks so grown up at the cash register.
She doesn't think she is somebody, but how could she cause
    me and others to feel so special if she is a nobody?
Lord, will she have the joy of knowing how much she gives
    when she smiles at a customer and asks, "How are you
    today?"
Will anyone help her connect what she does with who she is
    as your disciple? Are you asking me to be that someone?

I'm free. I'm free. I'm free. I passed my drivers test. I was so nervous. I thought I would fail, but you were with me. Thank you. Now I can drive. Now I can go places. Now I am on my way. My life will never be the same. Now I have a drivers license.

But with freedom comes responsibility. Responsibility for the others in my car, responsibility for those in cars I meet, responsibility for pedestrians I pass. Others may suffer if I make a mistake. Help me to drive safely. Let no harm come to others because of my actions. Lord, help me to sense your presence every time I turn on the ignition. As I guide the steering wheel, may I be open to your guidance in my life. Amen.

Loving Lord of life, let me take this time to offer up these prayers of concern amidst my busy workday:

For coworkers (*names*).

For the hard decisions I must make (*list*).

For the people affected by my work (*name*).

For specific work needs (*list*).

Gracious and merciful God, you have always been there for me through thick and thin, and I need your presence very much at this time. Losing one's job is like losing one's identity in our society, and you know well my hurt and sorrow at this particular time in my life. I worry about my financial situation. I worry about my reputation. I worry about what others will think of me. I worry about my prospects in finding a new job. I worry. I worry.

Help me to put this loss in perspective. Help me to understand that I am not totally at fault. Help me to see that there will be a new tomorrow. Help me to trust that something new will come along. My work is not my whole life; it is but a piece of my life. You are the foundation of my life, and I pray that I can live faithfully today and every day that you give me. I am alive, and that is more important than any job. There is a job that waits for me. Help me until that job comes. Amen.

O Lord, I am called by you alone. All my life is a calling. You call me to lead a faithful life. You call me to active discipleship. You call me to make a difference in your world. I realize that the people I work for and with, the products that I make or results that I deliver, are a part of my calling but not all my calling.

You have called me to live with compassion, forgiveness, and justice in all that I do in life. I am called to enable love, mercy, and righteousness to infuse my daily walk. In all that I do—work, family, play, and church—may my calling shine through like the dawning of each new day.

I pray this day to live your call from the time I awake until the time I lay down to sleep, filled with gratitude for the gift of one more day. Amen.

Through this computer, God, I am connected across the globe. With a push of a button and the moving of a mouse, I can talk to someone in London and leave messages for people in Egypt. Remind me, O God, that the Internet is not new. You made us one people long before computers were invented. Before phone lines stretched across the land or fiber-optic cables sent signals beneath our streets, we were already connected to one another, woven together by your great love. Amen.

O Lord, you know all things and you know the uncertainty I have in my heart. The future of my work is uncertain, as things are changing so rapidly in my job situation. Give me strength to face this uncertainty. Help me to cope with the pressures and anxiety that come with change. Give me a stronger faith in order to trust that you will make all things right.

I know that you give me the strength to go on with life. You provide the foundation of a new day; and with that new tomorrow, I will find my place in it. Calm the restlessness of my heart. There are new possibilities about to break forth in my life; and if I trust in you, they will become real. Amen.

Lord, I come to the end of a very busy day in the midst of a very busy week. I have felt at times like a circus clown, juggling so many elements into the air, performing my best but sometimes dropping items. Thrown into the air like juggling balls have been family, friends, work, study, exercise, travel, chores, church, and even leisure. The crowd expects me to perform at my best, and I give it my best shot; but sometimes I am overwhelmed. I drop balls, and the people around me are disappointed.

What I ask for now is the peace of rest. Allow me a deep and soothing sleep. Let my tired muscles rejuvenate overnight. Allow my brain to be set loose, uncontrolled, and allow my dreams to be creative and wonderful. Let my tired soul rest with your peace. Renew me with this sleep, and allow me to awaken fresh and regenerated. Amen.

Help me, O Lord, to be at my best during this coming meeting. Enable me to listen attentively, to be clear and concise in voice, and to think and reason clearly. Whether I am leading or being led in this meeting, enable me to contribute my unique position and point of view for the good of all. I ask for your strength in undergirding my participation. Thank you for being my center and enabling me to be at my best. Through Jesus your Son I pray. Amen.

The doctor hasn't called. I'm worried. I can think only of all the bad choices and options. I wish the doctor didn't have to call. I pray for good news, but I fear the worst. Give me the power and strength to endure.

You did not send this to me as a test or a punishment, but how I respond is a mark of who I am and how you have shaped me. Build up my immunity by building up my faith, for nothing can separate us. We will stand and fight and laugh and cry together. You will lend me your Spirit and hold me for support. I will honor you with my life. Amen.

Make this bed, O God, a sanctuary. May it always be a place of love where vows are honored and hopes are born, where passions are ignited, and where love will never reach its limits.

Make this bed, O God, a place of grace. May it be a place where, by our words and deeds, we forgive each other, speak and kiss tenderly with each other, promise to stay with each other, and in all things be loving with each other.

Make this bed, O God, sacred. May it be a place where abundant life is born, where new life is created, where old life is renewed and made fresh, where tired life finds purpose, where ordinary life finds new destiny, where half-remembered prayers are answered, where bedtime confessions are heard and new days begun.

Make this bed, O God, become holy by your presence. Be with us in our hugging and in our kissing. Be with us in our passion and in our tears. Be with us in our loneliness when the bed is empty. Be with us as we sleep and when the alarm wakes us. Be with us. Amen.

For Worship Planners

This resource focuses on the necessity of connecting worship and work so that the whole people of God live out their baptismal vocation of loving God and loving neighbor in daily life. Liturgy divorced from the everyday life is a lifeless mannequin. When worship connects everyday life and the gospel of Jesus Christ through Word and sacrament, people are affirmed and empowered with a clear identity as priests and servants in all the arenas of their daily life. Children playing and learning together, elderly people calling to check on one another's welfare and laughing about the trials of getting old, young people smiling at customers while taking orders at the local fastfood restaurant, and parents loving their children, all of these are examples of Christian ministry just as much as is the work of clergy and church professionals.

While we tend to equate worship with what happens in the sanctuary on Sunday morning, it is important to note that worship occurs in many different places. The writers of this book hope that this resource will be used in a wide variety of settings to help people understand themselves as faithful disciples wherever God places them. Leaders of small-group ministries will find prayers that can be used to gather the group and to send them forth. Church committees and other work teams will find resources to help those present connect the work of the group with the work of God. People who gather in small groups in the workplace for Bible study and prayer will find prayers and litanies to help them relate the realities of their world to the call of God in their lives.

This section aims to help you use the resources found in this and other books in the actual week-to-week task of developing worship. We will look at the work of worship planning that affirms people in their ministry in daily life and consider the roles of clergy and laity in planning and leading worship. We will reflect on the various calendars that shape worship connected to daily life: the Christian calendar (and lectionary); our civil, local, and cultural calendars and cycles; and our personal calendars and cycles. This section concludes with a list of hymns, prayers, and other components from selected contemporary hymnals and worship books.

The work of worship planners

Planning worship is an essential and critical part of the daily work of pastors, musicians, and other congregational leaders who are responsible for the Sunday liturgy of the people. The word *liturgy* means "the work of the people." The liturgy of the gathered community on Sundays continues in the world where the faithful live and work Monday to Sunday. To help members of the worshiping community understand that liturgy both points to and is part of their daily life requires careful preparation on the part of worship planners. This is especially true since ministry has frequently been understood as service to the church rather than what the baptized do as God's agents in God's world.

If worship is seven days a week, then corporate worship must be carefully planned to affirm that fact and to encourage those who will be sent out in Christ's ministry for the life of the world. Planning liturgy that calls people to live out their baptismal covenant is a high challenge and one that takes persistent attention to the choices of words and ritual texts, hymns and songs, prayers, leaders, gestures, architecture, art, and graphics used to shape the liturgy of the people.

Further, worship happens in the larger context of the congregation's life and vision. What is the vision of the congregation for itself? When new people come, how are they received? How do you and your congregation hope their lives will be shaped by participating in the worship and fellowship of your church? Will someone take time to know them and listen to their hopes and hurts? Will some members take time to listen to them tell about their daily life and work in home, community, workplace, leisure, and political life? Are there settings where youth and adults can journey together and hold one another in mutual care and accountability for resisting evil, trusting Christ, and serving as his representatives in the world? Are children who are baptized into Christ and his reign seen as members of Christ's royal priesthood? Are their engagements in play, school, family, and community affirmed as expressions of Christian vocation? Planning worship has to connect to the primary task of the congregation: to reach out and receive people as they are, relate them to God, nurture them in the faith, and send them out to live as disciples of Jesus Christ in witness where God is at work in the world.

The transformation of the world begins in and returns to the Word and sacraments lavishly proclaimed and enacted in spirit and in truth (see John 4:23). Liturgy, the public work of the people, is both formal and gathered, and informal and scattered. The weekly gathering of the disciples around the risen Christ is the "source and summit" of our life. Each week Christians gather around the table of Word and Eucharist, where we are called and transformed for living as apostles of love and mercy, justice and hope. Worshiping the Trinity is not a list of things we do, nor one activity among many; it is a holy communion with Jesus to the praise of God, the Father, in the power of the Spirit. There this triune God becomes the heartbeat of our own hearts as we are broken open for service and witness wherever the Spirit takes us.

Planning for this kind of transforming worship requires that those who plan and lead worship be continuously attentive to Christ and alert to the world and work of the worshipers. For it is these same worshipers who will be priests and ministers of the new covenant in the homes, schools, entertainment centers, government buildings, factories, corporate offices, hospitals, and shopping malls of the community.

The people, Christ's own body through baptism, are a priesthood. The New Testament and the early church never used the term *priest* to refer to an individual other than Christ. Jesus was their faithful high priest. They did, however, understand the whole community to be a priesthood (see 1 Peter 2:9). This is why in the baptismal liturgy the community welcomes the newly baptized into Christ's royal priesthood (see *The United Methodist Hymnal*, page 37, number 11). When the prayer of thanksgiving is prayed at the Communion, it is the whole community that offers itself to God as a sacrifice of praise and thanksgiving. Yes, the pastor presides; but it is the whole people who are giving thanks and praise and saying with unmistakable clarity,

> in remembrance of these your mighty acts in Jesus Christ,
> we offer ourselves in praise and thanksgiving
>> as a holy and living sacrifice,
>> in union with Christ's offering for us,
> as we proclaim the mystery of faith.

It is this whole people that the Spirit will make

>> . . . one with Christ,
>> one with each other,
>> and one in ministry to all the world.

Without an understanding of the people as Christ's royal priesthood, worship will continue to focus inward instead of outward. Without awareness and fresh appreciation of the struggles and dreams of those who worship, planners will likely allow the cosmic scope of Christ's ministry to collapse down to preserving the church as an institution focused on survival, and comforting the inner circle of its members. *Don't let that*

WORSHIP&
DAILY
LIFE

happen! Apostolic ministry unleashes and sustains the people in the venture of faith sharing and acts of justice and compassion in every corner of creation.

Planning for worship that is transformational is best done by teams. Your worship team may be only two or three people. Or it may include a core of five or six and a larger team of ten to twenty. It depends on the complexity of worship in your setting. The point is, you can't do this alone. To attempt to do so denies the gifts of those in your faith community who are able to connect God's praise to God's compassion and justice in the world. Here are some basic points to keep in mind as you participate in the planning process for the worship and witness of Christ's royal priesthood.

Keep worship sacramental

This means more than celebrating the sacraments of baptism and the Lord's Supper. When we say that something is sacramental, we mean that it connects us with God's grace. God acts in us to touch us and help us taste and see the goodness of God. By the grace of God, all of life is potentially sacramental. Actions, things, and relationships serve as means of seeing and tasting the grace of God. Real life is sacramental. Plan and lead worship to connect people with real life. Invite the deep look that welcomes insight and playful engagement with what we may have overlooked. Light, water, ashes, oil, bread, wine, people, hugs, laughter, fabric, confident leadership, vessels, and more are elements God uses to pour out blessings and gifts upon God's people. Be concrete, graphic; tell stories of real people.

Remember that people are seeking God

Worship is about encounter with God. Move from thinking of worship as a lecture—something to be understood—to worship as a relational engagement with God. Allow for the emotional side to be alive, and welcome the Holy Spirit to come and touch the people at the point of their deepest longings. Don't shy away from people's pain. Create settings and use resources that enable the people to name the pain (outward and social, and inward and personal) and hold it up to God in prayer so that it is transformed and redeemed.

Consider all of the people

What about children and youth? older adults? people with disabilities? What do the people struggle with in living faithfully in daily life? How could worship affirm them and the work and witness the Spirit is prompting in them?

Details, details, details

Every worship service is unique. Even if worship seems the same week after week, each service is different. Plan with the push of the past (Scripture, hymns and songs, and the fullness of Christian tradition) in mind and with the pull of the present and future (the hope and hurts of the people in their daily life) in mind.

Continuously improve

Bring about change by asking your worship planning and leadership team, What worked well in today's service? What could have been improved so that the primary task was lived out? What did we learn? This will not bring sudden change or dramatic improvement, but faithfully done, it will bring continuous growth in the quality of the community's liturgical life.

For further suggestions and guidance related to team planning see *Planning Vital Worship: 1997–2000* in the *Guidelines for Leading Your Congregation* series (Abingdon Press, 1996; order from Cokesbury, 1-800-672-1789).

The role of elders, deacons, and laity in affirming daily life ministry in worship

The work of specialized ministries in the church is never an end in itself; pastors, teachers, prophets, and evangelists are gifts from the church to the church "to equip the saints for the work of ministry, for building up the body of Christ" (Ephesians 4:12). From earliest times in the church, the Spirit has called and the church has ordered ministries of leadership so that the whole people of God would be equipped and supported in proclaiming and enacting the gospel for the transformation of the world. This equipping, leading, guiding work is essential to the health and effectiveness of the church's ministry, but it is never to be equated with the church's ministry.

The movement to recover a full-blown *diaconate* (order of deacons) may be a healthy push for the church in several ways. First, it pushes us to be more clear in our use of language. As noted in the Introduction of this book, the term *minister* is to be used inclusively of all who are baptized into Christ's way and life. Second, the emergence of deacons causes the church to ask itself, what is it that deacons are to do that is different from what elders do? What are the unique gifts and graces that God gives to elders and deacons? How can these two forms of ministry be distinctive, complementary, and equal in leading the body of Christ? How are their differing functions in leading the people to be mirrored in the Sunday gathering for worship.

WORSHIP&
DAILY
LIFE

Consider the following guidelines for understanding and exercising the relationship of elders (presbyters), deacons, and non-ordained people in leading worship. (Note: Denominations use varying terms for the presbyter, such as *elder* or *priest* or *teaching elder* or *pastor*. This book uses *presbyter* as an equivalent for those terms.)

Christ has only one ministry; presbyters and deacons are distinctive orders of ministry within this one ministry of Christ. The distinctiveness is grounded in God's calling and empowering the community to live out its baptismal vocation of unity and service.

The liturgical leadership roles of presbyters and deacons serve the church best when the distinctiveness is not glossed over but is enacted with clarity and charity in worship and witness. Mutual respect for the office and work of each order within the ministry of all Christians enables each order to mirror the nature and mystery of the whole church: Christ as priest and Christ as servant. The leadership of presbyters and deacons is for the sake of the whole church so that it may offer worship to God through Jesus Christ by the power of the Holy Spirit. Orders have no separate existence apart from the community of the baptized from which the ordained are called to serve.

The presbyter's liturgical function is to preside and unify at the assembly's celebration of Word and sacrament. Presbyters preserve the unity of the church in its baptismal and Eucharist life. Presbyters express Christ's royal priesthood that all Christians enter at baptism, and they oversee the life of the congregation so that people are reconciled and united to Christ throughout their lives. Their work and office might be symbolized by an encompassing circle.

The deacon's liturgical function is to link and extend the assembly's celebration of Word and sacrament to its service (*diaconia*) in daily life. The deacon lives, looks, and listens on the margins of human life and human need. Deacons live at the intersection of the good news celebrated at the gathered liturgy and the tragic news of the poor and oppressed. They lead the baptized in Christ's servanthood. Their work and office can be symbolized by a connecting line.

Since presbyters are ordained to service as well as to word, sacrament, and order, they are not exempt from linking liturgy and life in their presiding and proclaiming. Where there is no deacon, the presbyter will have to lead as both presbyter and deacon and utilize lay people as assisting ministers who carry out the deacon's role in worship.

Since they are ordained to word as well as service, deacons are not excused from faithful proclamation of the Word of God in worship as well as in daily life.

Presbyters most appropriately preside at the community's worship by greeting the assembly in the name of God, proclaiming and interpreting the Word of God in preaching, announcing God's forgiveness to the people (and receiving God's forgiveness from the people), presiding at the Eucharist, and blessing the people as they go forth into the world.

Deacons most appropriately lead in linking and extending Christ's service in the community's worship by reading the Scriptures, particularly the Gospel reading; preaching to interpret the hurts and hopes of the world; leading the people in prayers for the world and the church; receiving the elements and preparing the table for the Eucharist; assisting in serving the Communion; setting the table in order after all have been served; and sending the people forth to serve. Deacons may train and guide others to do these tasks or to assist in doing them.

It is worth noting that the Evangelical Lutheran Church in America consecrates diaconal ministers but has so far resisted ordaining deacons, in part for concern that the diaconate not be professionalized and clericized in either liturgy or life. This book, in keeping with ecumenical practice, strongly encourages that one or more members of the assembly serve as assisting ministers in reading the Scriptures, leading the people in prayer for the world and the church, preparing the table for Holy Communion, and sending the people forth in service.

The Christian calendar and lectionary

While all worship gatherings of the community around Word and sacraments are to be affirmations of the work of the whole people of God for the life of the world, there are some times on the calendar of the Christian year that invite a clear focus on the vocation to ministry in daily life. Each of the times listed below is ecumenically recognized as especially suited to celebration of the baptismal covenant. Since all ministry is Christ's ministry, days of renewing the baptismal covenant are also prime days for recalling our vocation to hallow God's name in all our living and labor.

Easter Vigil and Easter Day

Easter is the primordial day for Christians to recall our dying and rising with Christ in baptism. Hold baptisms and the renewal of baptism within the great festive joy of this triumph of God's life in the face of the injustice and oppression by the powers of evil. Let proclamation and liturgy be rich with God's delivering power that is at work in us in all of our contact with the powers of evil, injustice, and oppression that we are pledged to resist in our baptism.

The Great Fifty Days

Easter is fifty days of high celebration of the power of the Resurrection. "I am the resurrection and the life," is rehearsed again and again in these days. The readings, particularly those from the Acts of the Apostles, can be used to powerfully illustrate the risen Lord at work in ordinary women and men. Affirm the vocation of all Christians in song, liturgy, and sermon. If you hold confirmations during this time, or whenever you confirm people, ensure that the action is seen as God's strengthening individuals to live their profession of faith in daily life. Avoid confirmations that look like graduation ceremonies and that terminate worship and witness rather than unleash apostolic ministry for a lifetime.

Pentecost

As the conclusion of the Great Fifty Days, the Day of Pentecost is a feast of the manifold work of the Spirit. It culminates Easter and focuses on the outpouring of the Spirit upon the church for bold proclamation. Many congregations hold services of baptism and/or confirmation on this day. Avoid any hint of graduation, achievement, or completion. In preparation of those to be baptized or confirmed, focus on discovering each one's spiritual gifts and on discernment of vocation in Christ's mission in the world. It is also an excellent day for using "A Celebration of New Beginnings in Faith" (*The United Methodist Book of Worship*, pages 588–590).

The Baptism of the Lord

This is a prime day for baptism and the renewal of the baptismal covenant. Emphasize the connection beween Jesus' baptism and Jesus' testing before the choices he faced in the wilderness and his years of ministry. In sermon and liturgical action, connect the Spirit's descent on the baptized with the Christian identity and vocation of the whole people of God.

All Saints' Day

Here is a day for concrete illustration. Those who demonstrate for us what it means to be disciples in particular circumstances should be lifted up and celebrated. Visuals, stories, and invitations to remember those who have been representatives of Christ in our world should be highlighted in this day's liturgical celebration. All Saints' Day is another appropriate day for baptisms and the renewal of the baptismal covenant as we affirm and celebrate God's including us in the communion of saints. As with all of the previously mentioned days, this is a day for celebration of the sacrament of Holy Communion.

The civil and local calendars

Daily life is lived not only by a daily cycle (waking, working, resting, and meals) but by a calendar cycle of weeks and months. There are national days of observance, state and regional events, and local customs generated by the area's historical, cultural, and commercial life. Many of these serve as focal points for community life and may be meaningfully used for the connection of worship and work, liturgy and ministry.

The following are examples:

- New Year's Day (January 1)—naming Jesus as sovereign of all days, times, and places;
- Martin Luther King, Jr's., birthday (January 15)—committing ourselves to the ongoing work of ending racism and poverty and doing justice;
- Presidents' Day (third Monday in February)—recognizing and celebrating national leadership by historic figures;
- Mother's Day (May) and Father's Day (June)—affirming our love and appreciation for those who have birthed or adopted us into their families;
- Memorial Day (last Monday in May)—remembering those who gave their lives in war;
- Independence Day (July 4)—reflecting on the vision of our national life and affirming political and social engagement;
- Labor Day (first Monday in September)—celebrating the work of all people in contributing to the common good;
- The resumption of school classes in August/September—affirming the work of teachers and students;
- Thanksgiving (last Thursday in November) and harvest festivals—feasting and celebrating the goodness and abundance of God's provision and the wonder of our collaboration in the gift of creation;
- Fishing fleets going to sea—blessing the fishing fleets and recognizing the risk-taking of such work;
- Commencing of wheat harvest—blessing God for the gift of food and the means to obtain it in abundance.

This is only illustrative of the variety of particular days that can be tapped for heightening prayerful connection of the significance and vocational quality of daily living. Your local setting will have its own unique observances and ritual practices to which Christian worship speaks.

Personal calendars

Birthdays, anniversaries, the beginning of a new job, election of a person to public office, purchase and occupancy of a new home, and many other occasions can and should be marked by recognition, blessing, and prayer within the Sunday

service and in special celebrations. Engagement to be married, marriage, the birth of children, and death are times of profound experience and exploration of our Christian vocation grounded in baptism.

The Spirit calls congregational leaders to weave all such moments and observances into the ongoing liturgical life of the faith community. This resource is an invitation to imaginative and resourceful use of God's work in ongoing daily living.

Resources in this volume and in your congregation's existing worship resources

The resources in this volume are an attempt to model the kind of prayers and other acts of worship that could be used to help congregations experience affirmation and empowerment for their vocation of ministry in daily life. These are supplemental to many hymns, prayers, and other worship texts and actions that are admirably suited to meeting this need. What follows is a sampling from several prominent hymnals and books of worship used in mainline denominations. In no way should you see this as a complete listing, nor should you consult it alone in searching for hymns and other resources for affirming ministry in daily life. Use it as a tool, but by all means make your own search. One of the values of these listings is recognition that there are a wide range of sources for your congregation's use.

Of course there are copyright issues that must be observed. Be sure to check the source for the permissions and restrictions that apply. (See the imprint page of this book for information on using pieces from this book.) Some books allow for local, one-time use as long as the proper credit line and permission notice are printed with the use. If the source forbids copying for use in your context, there are several ways to get permission that are legal and fair. For a one-time use of a specific hymn or prayer, write or call the publisher and ask what the arrangements and costs are for a one-time use. Even if there is a cost, it is likely to be modest and reasonable. If you discover that you will want to use other resources from time to time or frequently, inquire about licensing arrangements through CCLI, LicenSing, G.I.A., or other group licensing companies. Here are several sources for licensing arrangements.

CCLI (Christian Copyright Licensing, Inc.): 17201 NE Sacramento Street, Portland, OR 97230, phone 1-800-234-2446.

This is a licensing company for over 2,500 music publishers. Securing an annual license from CCLI allows a church to copy songs for congregational use, including printing in orders of service and on overhead transparencies, and audio and video recording of services. Call for complete information.

LicenSing: 6160 Carmen Avenue East, Inver Grove Heights, MN 55076, phone 1-800-328-0200.

Aimed at resourcing mainline, ecumenical, liturgical churches, this company provides copyright clearance, access tools, cross-reference of titles, and a quarterly periodical, *Update*, that highlights music for use with the Revised Common Lectionary texts. Call for sign-up and cost information.

G.I.A: 7404 South Mason Avenue, Chicago, IL 60638, phone 1-800-442-1358.

G.I.A. provides all styles of Christian music resources. It publishes a large number of contemporary music resources that are useful in churches that follow the calendar of the Christian year and the lectionary.

Movie and video clip use

Increasing numbers of churches are helping people connect the gospel and ministry in daily life by using video clips as part of the sermon or in some other part of the liturgy. If you do this or plan to do this, you should be aware of the following information.

Copyright restrictions apply to video formats for films. The opening words of commercial videos indicate that the tape is intended for "home use only." Legally, this excludes use in churches, either for worship or for viewing by a group in the church, such as youth fellowship. As with the music licensing companies, you may purchase a license that will allow you to legally use videotapes of popular films in your church. The license will allow you to show a video in its entirety, or scenes from a video, but not to edit or copy it in any way. Modest fees are based on the anticipated viewing audience. In order to obtain permission, contact Church Desk, Motion Picture Licensing Corporation, 58 Jeremiah Road, Sandy Hook, CT 06482, phone 1-800-515-8855.

Resources in hymnals

Most late-twentieth-century hymnals contain numerous hymns and songs that link faith and worship of God to the places and people we live with during the week. Commonly used hymnals and their abbreviations for the chart on the following pages include

The United Methodist Hymnal (UMH), United Methodist, 1989;

Lutheran Book of Worship (LBW), Evangelical Lutheran Church in America, 1979;

The Hymnal 1982 (H82), The Episcopal Church, 1985;

The New Century Hymnal (NCH), United Church of Christ, 1995;

The Presbyterian Hymnal (PH), Presbyterian Church (U.S.A.), 1990;

With One Voice: A Lutheran Resource for Worship (WOV), supplement to *The Lutheran Book of Worship*, 1995;

Lead Me, Guide Me: The African American Catholic Hymnal (LMGM), The Roman Catholic Church, 1987;

RitualSong: A Hymnal and Service Book for Roman Catholics (RS), The Roman Catholic Church, 1996.

There are many other current hymnals that could have been cited. The chart on pages 108 and 109 is illustrative and limited by space. Its intent is to illustrate the kinds of hymns and songs available for worship planners who seek to select hymns that affirm and support the connection of liturgy with ministry in daily life. If your hymnal is not listed, check its indices to determine if these hymns and songs are included in it.

Because of its particular focus on ministry in daily life, we list one additional work not in hymnals: Philip R. Dietterich's musical *The Ministry of All Christians* (Agape, 1976).

Resources in books of worship

As with the listing of hymns, the list of prayers and blessings on page 110 is illustrative rather than exhaustive. Care should be taken to explore these and other books of worship resources for suitable liturgical texts related to ministry in daily life.

The volumes sampled are

The United Methodist Book of Worship (UMBOW), United Methodist, 1992;

The United Methodist Hymnal (UMH), United Methodist, 1989;

The Book of Common Prayer (BCP), The Episcopal Church, 1979;

Book of Common Worship (BCW), Presbyterian Church (U.S.A.) and the Cumberland Presbyterian Church, 1993;

Book of Blessings (BB), The Roman Catholic Church, 1989.

Written prayers and ritual texts are gifts of the whole church. They are resources that shape Christian prayer and link us to the regional, global, and historic church as we pray and bless the work of Christ in the events of our daily lives. Use of these and other texts should not be slavish. These are models that invite adaptation for the particular circumstances in which they are to be prayed. Worship planners and leaders will find here resources that model the style and manner of prayer and blessing that invite their own efforts in crafting liturgical texts. Adapt these prayers or create new ones as needed for occasions and settings affirming and empowering the ministry of Christians in the demands and opportunities of their daily living.

A select list of resources for worship planning, connecting prayer and worship with daily life

Book of Blessings (The Liturgical Press, 1989).

Book of Common Worship (Westminster/John Knox Press, 1993).

Lead Me, Guide Me: The African American Catholic Hymnal (G.I.A. Publications, Inc., 1987).

Lutheran Book of Worship (Augsburg Publishing House and Board of Publication, Lutheran Church in Amerca, 1978).

Ritual Song: A Hymnal and Service Book for Roman Catholics (G.I.A. Publications, Inc., 1996).

The Book of Common Prayer (The Seabury Press, 1979).

The Hymnal 1982 (The Church Hymnal Corporation, 1985).

The New Century Hymnal (The Pilgrim Press, 1995).

The Presbyterian Hymnal (Westminster/John Knox Press, 1990).

The United Methodist Book of Worship (The United Methodist Publishing House, 1992).

The United Methodist Hymnal (The United Methodist Publishing House, 1989).

With One Voice: A Lutheran Resource for Worship (Augsburg Fortress, 1995).

RESOURCES IN HYMNALS	UMH	LBW	H82	NCH	PH	WOV	LMGM	RS
Make Me a Channel of Your Peace (prayer of St. Francis)								830
O for a World (envisioning a new world order)				575	386			
O Grant Us, God, a Little Space (work and prayer)				516				
O Young and Fearless Prophet	444							
Only What You Do for Christ Will Last (choices in daily life, serving Christ)							286	
Praise With Joy the World's Creator				273				
Pray for the Wilderness (care of creation, ecojustice)				557				
Pues Si Vivimos/When We Are Living	356			499	400			727
Sent Forth by God's Blessing (sending out)	664	221						
Shine, Jesus, Shine (vision, Transfiguration)						651		
Spirit of Jesus, If I Love My Neighbor				590				
Take My Gifts (Eucharist imagery)				562				
Take Up Thy Cross	415	398	204					808
The Church of Christ, in Every Age (servant life)	589	433			421			
The Spirit Sends Us Forth to Serve (sending)						723		
The Summons/Will You Come and Follow Me								811
The Voice of God Is Calling	436							
There's a Spirit in the Air (Eucharist imagery)	192			294	433			689
Those Who Love and Those Who Labor (mystery of Christ in work)								805
Tú Has Venido a la Orilla/Lord, You Have Come to the Lakeshore	344		173	377	784		116	817
We All Are One in Mission (sending, commitment)					435	755		
We Are Not Our Own (Eucharist, work of care)				564				
We Are Your People (prayer for faithfulness in daily life)					436			
We Cannot Own the Sunlit Sky (common labor for justice)				563				
When Jesus Came Preaching (discipleship then and now)								773
When Love Is Found (marriage vocation)	643			362		749		
Womb of Life, and Source of Being				274				
World Without End (the ordinary struggles of life)								673

RESOURCES IN BOOKS OF WORSHIP	UMBOW	UMH	BCP	BCW	BB
Baptismal vocation: life with the church in ministry	81, 86	33	299	403–430	
Baptismal covenant day: baptism of the Lord	299			198	
Baptismal covenant day: Easter vigil	369		285	294	
Baptismal covenant season: Easter	377			315	
Baptismal covenant day: Pentecost	405			338	
Baptismal covenant day: All Saints' Day	413			385	
Reaffirmation/confirmation of the baptismal covenant	111	50	299	447	
Interceding for the world of daily life	495			99–120	
Blessings (UMBOW and BB) and prayers:					
for birthdays	533		830	826	100
for a Quinceañera	534				
for beginning of a new school year	535		824		179
for graduates	536				
for an engaged couple	537			822	59
for families			841	822	3
for beginning a new job	538				
for disciples in the marketplace	539			820	
for those who work	540				
for travelers			831	836	219
for those who are unemployed	541		824	837	
for harvest of lands and waters			828	801	
for those in military service	542		823	818	
for the beginning of retirement	543				
for leisure			825	831	
for an election			822	817	
for leaders	544			816	
for local government			822		
for organizations concerned with public need					201
for towns and rural areas			825		
for cities			825	820	
for the neighborhood				821	
for those who suffer	545				
for the poor and neglected			826		
for prisons and correctional institutions			826		
for those who live alone and single people			829	824	
for families with one parent				827	
for the care of children			829		
for the sexually confused				835	
for a victim or survivor of crime	546				141
on the anniversary of a death	548				
for animals (October 4 or other time)	608				347
for a home	610				237
for an office, shop, or factory					293
for boats and fishing gear					323
New beginnings in faith	588				
Commitment to Christian service	591				
Charge to the people/Sending out	31, 39, 559			159–160	
Vocation: marriage	115	864	423	841	
Vocation: family	437, 585		439		

Contributors

This volume was developed by a team of gifted writers who are committed to a vision in which all of life is worship.

Chestina Mitchell Archibald, longtime chaplain at Fisk University, is now pastor of Braden United Methodist Church in Nashville, Tennessee. As an outstanding inspirational and motivational speaker she has spoken at universities such as Harvard, Howard, Duke, and Vanderbilt. She is the editor of *Say Amen: The African-American Family's Book of Prayers* (Dutton) and coeditor of *Divine Inspirations: Pearls of Wisdom From the Old and New Testaments* (HarperCollins). She is a native of Thomasville, Georgia, and the mother of one son, I. Albert John Archibald.

Daniel Benedict is Worship Resources Director for the General Board of Discipleship of The United Methodist Church. He is an elder in the California-Pacific Annual Conference. Dan is the author of *Come to the Waters* (Discipleship Resources) and the coauthor of *Contemporary Worship for the 21st Century* (Discipleship Resources). He passionately advocates the affirmation of Christian vocation as ministry in daily life and the unleashing of the laity for apostolic witness and service.

Diane Luton Blum is an elder in the Tennessee Annual Conference of The United Methodist Church. She is a graduate of Oberlin College and Vanderbilt Divinity School. She and her husband, Jeff Blum, are the parents of two teenage sons. Currently Diane serves as one of the pastors at First United Methodist Church in Franklin, Tennessee. Diane's ministry interests include urban ministry, biblical studies, and spiritual formation.

Ray Buckley is the director of Native American Communications at United Methodist Communications in Nashville, Tennessee. He teaches a mid-week Sunday school class of mentally retarded adults and works with the homeless in the Nashville area. Ray is a member of Antioch United Methodist Church. He is also the author and illustrator of *God's Love Is Like* and *The Giveaway* (Abingdon Press). Ray has a fervent belief that every person and culture has unique gifts to

WORSHIP&
DAILY
LIFE

contribute to the body of Christ and that our greatest opportunity is in helping individuals release those gifts into our communities.

Paul Escamilla is an elder in the North Texas Conference of The United Methodist Church. He is a graduate of Candler School of Theology and serves as the pastor of Walnut Hill United Methodist Church in Dallas, Texas. Paul is the author of *Seasons of Communion* (Discipleship Resources) and has written numerous articles related to worship.

Alyne JoAnn Catolster is the director of Ministry in Daily Life and Community/Justice Ministries at the General Board of Discipleship of The United Methodist Church. She is an enrolled member of the Eastern Band of Cherokee Indians of Cherokee, North Carolina. JoAnn is committed to helping clergy and laity recognize and celebrate the ways that they live as disciples in everyday life.

Grant Hagiya is an elder in the California-Pacific Annual Conference of The United Methodist Church. He is a graduate of Claremont School of Theology and serves as the pastor of Centenary United Methodist Church in Redondo Beach, California. Grant has written Sunday school curriculum for The United Methodist Church.

Barbara Snell McLain is an elder in the Kansas West Conference of The United Methodist Church. She is a graduate of Perkins School of Theology and has served churches since 1982. Barbara is known for her story-sermons and her unique worship style. She and her husband, Allen, live in Ransom, Kansas, with their three children, Ryan, Christopher, and Kara.

Doris Johnson Rudy plans, implements, and administers the continuing education program at Garrett-Evangelical Theological Seminary, Evanston, Illinois. She recruits and trains Communion servers at First United Methodist Church; chairs the committee that recruits, trains, and deploys three hundred volunteers for First Night Evanston; and organizes Evanston's First Ward for her political party. She is friend and parent of one adult daughter.

Mark Wiley, a pastor in Lakewood, California, is known for writing creative prayer and liturgies. Nicknamed Word Dancer and Word Smith, Mark artistically expresses traditional theology in non-traditional images in order to make God more visible. A California native, Mark graduated from San Diego State and Claremont School of Theology. The great joys of his life are his wife, Jan, who is also a pastor, and his kids, Melissa and Nicholas.

Aileen Williams is a laywoman living in Rochester, Minnesota. Helping the church address discipleship issues is of key importance to her as she participates in the local congregation and the general church.